RAISING CONSCIOUSNESS

—

PREPARING FOR CHANGE

Part One

Extraterrestrial Guidance

for a Better Future

Elaine J Thompson

Ann Matkins

DEDICATION

Elaine Thompson

This book is dedicated to all the Extraterrestrial friends and Spiritual Guides who have loyally supported me with guidance and given me courage throughout my entire life. With their words of wisdom and encouragement, I see there is now hope and joy for the future of Earth and humanity. We must acknowledge that we are all Equal, all One, and all about to experience Change. My grateful thanks go to all my Extraterrestrial guides from so many star systems, and most of all to Lamgan and his family from the Andromedan Galaxy.

Ann Matkins

I would echo Elaine's words, that we hold so much gratitude towards our Extraterrestrial friends and guides for visiting us and sharing their messages of hope, wisdom and knowledge. Through my friendship with Elaine I have had the opportunity to meet new friends and new guides, to know their stories; and I'm always eager to hear the new knowledge they come to impart and share. I do so admire their understanding as they try with patience to demonstrate concepts that our everyday minds sometimes grasp with difficulty. They persevere because both Elaine and I believe, as our guides do, that the vital messages they bring are so important for all the peoples of Earth, and subsequently for our collective future.

CONTENTS

1   **Awareness is the Key:** An evolutionary leap of   1
    consciousness and awareness. Coming into alignment with
    the new energy and vibration coming to Earth now.

2   **The Antarctic and our Connectedness to the Planet:**   20
    Reconnection with Earth and our relationship with
    Nature.

3   **Domed Cities of the Future:** Lamgan talks about new   31
    technology that will create the cities of the future.

4   **The Future and the Past:** Changes to come that will   53
    affect our daily working lives.

5   **A Message from The Lyran:** How a quiet, unruffled   61
    mind can steer us through an uncomplicated life.

6   **July 2010: The Galactic Nations** gather to discuss a   68
    rogue Asteroid and a possible outcome for Earth.

7   **Macro and Micro:** The Birth of a Universe witnessed,   81
    and the Beginning of a New Age.

8   **A Touch of Light and freedom for the spirit on Earth.** 104
    A native American Indian speaks of brotherhood for the
    people of Earth.

9   **Joy to the World, the balance is tipped!** A time of Peace 122
    and Joy that is promised for the future.

10 **Angels, the Sound of Earth and connectedness of all**   132
    planets. The Core sound of Earth, A spaceship appears.

Prologue: March, 2017

Elaine and I always began our evenings together with a welcome prayer at the beginning of each session. It was a statement of our intent, and our insurance policy that our door was only open to those we wished to invite in. We never knew what the outcome would be for each evening, or knew ahead of time who would bring their knowledge and wisdom. Sometimes they would remind us of what we knew but didn't put into daily practice – a very human trait – but mostly they came to give us a deeper understanding of the world, the Galaxy and the Universe we live in.

Our interplanetary friends were able to surprise and excite our minds with messages that seemed so clear, and yet sometimes weren't so easy to put into practice – or into words. They helped us to understand and believe that we could take everyday life and reality into our own hands and make it everything we wanted it to be. Not an easy concept for humans to believe!

So with the same excitement we experienced when we were first receiving the information in 2010, we now present this account of all that was given to us, as it is now so relevant to the changes taking place on our Earth all around us, right now. Our wish is that all who read it will feel inspired to take personal responsibility and flow with the changes happening now, and those that will come in the near future. Raising our consciousness both individually and together, we can all create a collective future reality filled with Joy, Happiness, and lasting Peace.

Ann Matkins

CHAPTER 1

Awareness is the Key
Session One

Back in 2010, myself Ann and were strongly prompted by our Extraterrestrial friends to get together, in order to begin receiving communication from them once again. I was then living some distance away from Ann, feeling unsettled and wanting change. I was going through a tough period of transition, and not enjoying the energy of my small home, or its location.

Ann and I met weekly at her house, in the quiet rural town of Glastonbury, in England, where the energy from Earth is particularly strong, and where being in telepathic contact with all the loving Guides from our spirit realms, Extraterrestrial friends from distant star systems, and the Andromedan Galaxy, is made easier.

* * *

We open with a prayer:

Elaine: I think one of the Andromedans I have connected with before would like to say something for a short while. It's the father of Ptplec – Ptlamganenon*.

(*This name is my understanding of the sounds or tonal language that I felt when asking for his name. Andromedan names are not spoken words such as we use, but rather feelings given tonally. I only use names for ease of identification. I will refer to him as Lamgan in future text.)

Lamgan: We have been away from you for what seems like a long while, whilst you have been caught up in the pursuits of material living and passing from day to day, doing what you must in order to straighten out your energy. It is now time to really let material things go, on a certain level. This does not mean giving everything away and just sitting down and waiting. What I mean is, not to place so much emotional importance and attachment on material things.

For the time being, during the flow of energy that you are coming into alignment with right now, the most important thing on your human agenda should be to align your vibrational frequencies with *that which will come*, and that which is coming now. In short, to be much more in tune with the less distinct subtle energy that is all around you; and if that means spending more time sitting, walking in nature, contemplating, thinking, writing, and less time washing the dishes and scrubbing the floors (although he says there is nothing wrong with that), then so be it. It all boils down to your emerging awareness of what is already there but has previously been unseen and unfelt; and where your internal focus of attention is. So, whilst you are doing tasks that you need to do in daily life, be mindful to keep your focus of attention on the energy all around you and within you. Be more aware of your passing emotions and thoughts. Take time to see what arises in you, in your interactions with daily life, with people and situations – and your response to it, both emotionally and physically.

All the things we have taught you before about your five human senses and the five that extend from those – your energy antennae, as it were – these must now be put into daily use. Listen more closely, feel more deeply, take time to take in the aromas around you and linger with them for a moment longer. Use your eyes to see past what you think is there, and look for subtle colour or energy fields, feeling the joy of a new taste, or remembering the pleasure a child takes with bubbles, or sand. Let it be more included as a part of your world, a new appreciation of *all* that is around you; even the strength and fortitude of a lonely weed pushing its way through the concrete.

Be in awe of diversity and strength in nature. This will raise the level at which your physical body and cellular structure vibrates, entraining you to match the new dimension that has always been there. This is the very same dimension that resonates with all you are seeking now. It's the place where a better, more loving and peaceful world exists, where everything feels right.

Elaine: He is talking about the energy points on the body now (see: 'To Andromeda and Beyond', Chapter 6: The Ultimate Power of the Heart), and being able to use the heart as a magnifier for intention and energy. So, clearly, we have to spend less time with our electronics, computers, phones and distractions, and more time placing our awareness within into the heart area, and to our energetic sensors.

I am excited to know that we all have access to *such power*! To change the way we are in this world; to take an evolutionary leap of consciousness and awareness, and to be able to feel and use all the benefits that come with it. Who wouldn't want to live in a more peaceful, less stressed environment, and to see life and living in a totally different way? I would!

Lamgan: Sensing earthquake activity, coming rain, weather patterns and Earth changes, should be a most natural thing to you, but so often you are taken by surprise with the weather. Animals, birds and all other living things (except humans) are acutely attuned to this as part of their lives – it is as natural as breathing to them. I am aware that several times over the last week or so you, Elaine, have had strong impulses to do things and yet not done them. You have ignored your extended senses and dismissed them. I see that people do this with their children too, when they tell young children they are making things up, or imagining. Don't you know what these pictures and feelings are? They are your extended senses at work, showing you what is *also* there. You create fear, as if you were living life in a past dark age of no knowledge, and so you have shut down your ability to expand and be aware. In your distant past such people who saw and spoke about other dimensions and realms were imprisoned or put to death. But you are in a different age now, entering a new dimension of existence, with possibilities that will change your lives for the better in so many ways. The time has come for you to recognise that all your fear is self-created *by you*, and you must also know that you can perpetuate it, or you can let go of false beliefs that do not serve you, and change. This is always as you wish. But evolution and survival requires change, and so it must be.

Elaine: Yes, today I felt very strongly to take time and tune into my heart resonance, and I didn't, I put it off. I was doing emails and this, that, and the other, and I totally forgot. Lamgan said it would have helped me tonight to be more closely attuned to him.

Lamgan: What can I tell you that you do not already know? In terms of the planetary shifts, it won't be quite as bad as you think it might be – bad enough, but not as cataclysmic as some prophecies predict. The really big difference comes in the subtle energy changes.

You have those people who talk about Ascension and going into the Fifth Dimension. How can you be aware of that – those other dimensions – without your sensory antennae turned on? To have them turned on you need to be aware of them. As you know, energy flows where your attention goes, so it is so important for you to be focused and aware of your own energy and the energy around you. And within that, so many things will change. You talk of your law of attraction and your law of manifestation, but if you are trying to make that work without awareness and without using the power of intention properly then you cannot expect good results.

Elaine: I understand that Lamgan is reiterating what I already mentally know, but just reminding me that there is only one way to manifest this new dimensional energy and to actually join or resonate with it. It is actually there anyway, but to be able to merge with it is to take personal responsibility and pay attention to ourselves. Live it with awareness, and BE it.

Ann: Does he give us any other clues as to how we can improve our awareness? Is it only regular meditation practice?

Lamgan: Ann, monitor your thoughts more often, and notice them when you are doing tasks like gardening or looking after your plants. Particularly, I see you bending down over there in your garden, and first of all *not being aware* of the thoughts that cross your mind that are *not* concerned with the plants. Secondly, other thoughts that may be of a negative nature, like 'I don't know how I will do that, or 'That will probably be difficult'.

Ann: Is he saying to focus completely on what you are doing, rather than allowing your thoughts to drift to other things that have no connection to what you are involved with right now?

Elaine: Yes, be aware of your thoughts more often. Your left brain, or logical aspect of mind, is the part of you that will dig up any old problem to solve and keep you busy with it, and I must add that this is not the same as your greater consciousness. The part you have to monitor is your logical, problem-solving left brain. If you set your intention to really be in the Now moment, *where there are no problems*, then that aspect of your mind will be quiet.

Ann: Oh, I'm having so much trouble with that right now!

Elaine: Yes, we chew over our perceived problems a million times in a day, trying to find a solution. Whereas if you tell your problem-solving, thinking mind to be quiet, your higher consciousness will provide all the answers to any given situation.

Ann: I do believe that. My mind and thoughts have become very random lately, and I am really cross with myself that what I thought I had achieved a few years ago, has suddenly disappeared. I don't know if it's the turmoil of everything around us that I've become caught up in again – and allowed it – or whether this is teaching me the lesson that I don't really know how to be more disciplined, and I've got to go on learning.

Elaine: Well, Lamgan tells me that there's a phrase I used the other day which is quite relevant. When thoughts come into your mind that are not positive, are not carefree, he says:

Lamgan: Just say to your constantly worrying mind, 'Behind me with those thoughts! Everything is fine right now'.

I don't have to know the answers.

I don't have to know the reasons why.

In fact it holds me back to think about finding the answers by looking 'outside', because the real answers are all inside of me anyway.

Ann: I know. But people have said to me: 'It's all very well somebody saying 'live in joy', for instance, or 'think positively' – they say they're finding that is almost impossible with the way their life is. So you have to change part of your life, I suppose?

Lamgan: All perceived problems arise from fear, as I said before. All this needing to solve what seem like insurmountable problems, arise from the fear of what you think the consequences of those problems might be; whereas, in fact, if you always focus on the belief that 'everything is fine', it *will* work out – even though you may not know *how* it will work out. It will all be fine. And that gives energy in the *right direction* – matching your frequency to the good outcome. It's an inner knowing that everything is in perfect order, and not allowing your thinking mind to create different scenarios, such as: It could go wrong this way; it could go wrong that way; or perhaps it would change or go away if I did this?

Meet the perceived problems when they are standing in front of you in the Now moment, and do not try to meet perceived problems when they are weeks away or days away, as they may not even arrive at all. They may not be real, and if you pour energy into trying to solve something that may not be real (i.e. you think it could or it *might* happen), you are actually creating the scenario you don't want and giving it life and energy.

In fact if you follow this principle of focus in the Now, and that all is fine, the problems will never arise, because by constantly telling yourself that everything will work out fine, those things perceived as problems no longer *become* problems. For example, Ann, you were talking about publishing books, and so on. Don't think about that – that is not an issue that matters one jot right now.

All that matters is in this moment, and what is transpiring for you to be able to use at some point in the future. In fact we hope that you will begin to use it immediately, which is why we come to remind you, because you already know all of these things. Human beings in general need to take much more control of the conscious mind, and the habitual problem-solving mode that it runs in.

Ann: I think that's right. We feel we always have to have a problem-solving part of our brain that is constantly there working out what we need to do next in order to make life better. But actually it just makes it worse, because we get entangled in our thoughts, with no time or space left for inspiration or intuition.

Lamgan: Trying to problem solve excessively creates 'wrong' body chemistry (that of stress and worry), when in actual fact you are born as instinctual beings. You know instinctively how to suck, how to walk, how to crawl, how to speak. You learn by the tones of others which language you must speak, but it is in your instinctive nature that you can use all parts of yourselves. And also within you now, is an intuitive knowing of what must be done next to deal with anything you are presented with. By allowing the thinking conscious mind (which connects to the perceived fight or flight mechanism, and also to the love and joy mechanism too) to be quiet and stand back for a moment, you will experience an entirely new flow to the way you go about things in your life. *A new flow.* Consider this: It's like stepping from the muddy side pool that you have been standing in for years, into a clear running river flow that has no boundaries, no beginning, and no end. You can now sail along, having no idea if there will be a branch around the next corner, or a stone that you could stand on, but trusting that one will come. And when you do find your place to stop, you can hold there for a while and explore, whilst still surrendering to the flow of the water, and all is well, and perfect for you, every time.

Ann: Thank you. That's really good advice. What would you say to somebody who says that they have tried to live according to what you've just suggested, and still nothing goes right for them?

Lamgan: Then they must look inside, self-examine, and find those parts of themselves which constantly create the perceived need to have a fear-based protection mechanism in place. As an example, I will speak about money. The need for money is instilled in you as of paramount importance on this planet, because you can only see and think for the time being that it equals survival. When you create a fear of lack, or a perceived notion that there will never be enough money – *then so will it be.* You will manifest exactly that in order to prove to yourself again and again that your conscious mind is right. By thinking that money entails very hard work for you, or it's difficult to ever have enough – you will make it so.

If you come across people who have tried to do all these things and still nothing works, then they must find out what drives them from inside the conscious mind, and discover what their basic core beliefs are within the subconscious mind. Clear and honest self-examination for negativity and motivation; self-awareness of deepest beliefs, and the monitoring of your thoughts as we suggested earlier on, will help your understanding. You can then be aware of perpetual patterns that block the flow. For a human being, it takes practice to really be aware of all those hundreds of thoughts that go through your mind, minute by minute. You have to recognise *what* you are holding on to, in order to let go of it.

Ann: Can I ask another question? Often people feel that they have to suffer; they feel guilt. Therefore, a life that is abundant, joyful and full is not in their paradigm. It's not consciously what they feel they can have or even deserve, because surely life must be a struggle. That's how some people see it, and so these are the people who might do everything they are told that should change all of that – and it still doesn't work. Is that because of the resistance that you were describing then, that something inside them has to be dissolved, re-educated, or re-patterned?

Lamgan: Absolutely. If you believe life is a struggle, you will look around you and that is what will be reflected back to you. You see other people struggling, you see various scenarios of X = Y and A = B, and so on. If you have no money then you may think you will have nowhere to live. And so *you therefore create it*, because as you think and perceive so shall it be. This principle is equally true for the creation of the means to live your life as you really want it to be.

Ann: I think it is a hard concept for humans to grab hold of and to actually keep it going for the rest of their lives, because there are always so many little dips in life. Losing the trust that everything is perfect and will be so – no matter what appears to be in front of you right at that moment – can happen when the first thing that goes wrong brings back the belief that 'I can't do this', or 'I *knew* that would happen!' You hear that. Or: 'It doesn't work for me; it works for other people, but not for me'.

Lamgan: There are several things to say here. First of all, what arises in that scenario is your initial judgement as to whether some 'thing' or situation is good or bad, right or wrong; and, secondly, if you are wise enough, self-responsibility arises and asks you, 'How, and with what thoughts, did I create this – and what can I learn from it?'

And if you, as Elaine has done, start to go along an avenue in which you are met with nothing but block after block, or disaster after disaster, then know that this is your inner, creative self saying: 'This is the wrong path to take, don't go down that path. This way is not resonating with your soul energy, and your purpose'. Do not say to yourself that the situation was wrong, or that it was terrible, say: 'Thank you for the signs. I must come back to my inner self and re-evaluate in order to become aware of what I should do. And if I really think I want that thing that is being blocked, then maybe it will come later, or there is another way. Or perhaps the way I've been attempting to do it is not the best way to do it, so that it manifests easily'.

Ann: Evaluate seems like a good word. If you can see something is not working, then, as you say, you go back to basics and say: 'How am I doing this, and how can I do it differently?' So that would be evaluation.

Lamgan: It's the same principle as: If you want a plant to grow, you know you have to give it water and soil. If it fails to thrive then you must learn to go back to the beginning with a new plant, and care and water it differently.

Ann: Nurture it differently, give it different soil?

Lamgan: You may also at one point say: 'Well I don't think I really *want* to be a gardener', in which case you can stop, and go in another direction. But if you really love plants and gardening, and you truly want to continue with that path, then sit quietly and tune in to yourself and the plants. If you were totally resonating with your heart and inner feelings, *and* using your awareness, giving energy and love to the plant, then it would thrive anyway. *Trust yourself.* Be at one with your plants; love them as you would your children.

Ann: And your loving energy would help the plants, too.

Lamgan: Exactly. It's just the same with life, money, jobs, houses – with everything. First you must have a desire: a want *from your heart* to have something, do something, or create something. Do not think with the logical mind: 'How can I have this?' – think with the heart: 'I really want this', and then let it go. Allow yourself to flow along in this river of heart thoughts and watch it come to you. Then, immerse yourself in the emotions of the joy that you feel when you imagine having a thing or situation you desire. Don't try to manipulate; follow your intuition and allow.

This has been spoken about so many times in the writings called: The Law of Attraction. What people tend to do is to use the left side of the brain (as you see it), the conscious, logical mind. Thinking that constantly repeating a desire or want as a mental mantra will bring it into being is totally coming from the wrong place. You cannot create and manifest from logical will, this will confine you to the will of others and will keep you static.

True manifestation comes from your feelings, from the heart. You have to first believe that whatever it may be is now coming to you, then let go of trying. Feel the joy and anticipation, and watch what will happen. Then let everything that happens be ok, however it may manifest. Remember the whole picture is never revealed, so you cannot judge one part of the whole in any way. You do not box-in the given thing or concept; do not give it edges and make it rigid – allow it to morph and flow. So, for Elaine, if she would love a house of her own, she can imagine and picture the house, but I know I hear her say: 'Well I don't know how I'm ever going to get that, I haven't got enough money, I haven't got this or that', and so forth. That is her conscious mind chewing over the 'how' and the 'why' of the perceived problems. I remind her to put those thoughts to one side and see what you will have, or what you wish to be one with.

Elaine: I see myself not so much visualising the exterior walls of the house I would love, but I see myself in a garden, loving the plants, planting and tending. I see myself painting the walls, I see myself lighting the fire, because that's Love; that's the kind of love I would like to have in the house. It is not the house *per se*; it is the energy that I want to create within it. But I do very often revert to my thinking about how on earth can I get it, and to be honest, I haven't got a clue. So this is not only good advice for me, but also for anyone – and it all comes back to the very first point he made about being more *still* and *focused*, and spending less time with electronics and housework.*

(*Elaine's note: I have a wonderful new home now, just as I pictured! Next step, creating a house of my own that could hold my entire family, with every last detail I envisage being there.)

Lamgan: You can, of course, still do your daily tasks, but be more still inside, be more aware, and use those awareness antennae we talked about. Follow those sudden thoughts, those sudden whims that you get (I feel he is talking directly to me) about doing things, because it really changes the flow and the direction of your energy. It changes the things you create, *and* the final outcomes.

Elaine: In fact he must have heard me the other day (and he is reminding me now), talking about a Harry Potter film. The example is a magic potion that Harry Potter has called *Liquid Luck*. He has something to accomplish, but it seems like an impossible task. So he drinks the Liquid Luck and his friends tell him to go and do what they think is right, but his intuition says: 'No, no, don't go there; go here'. To the dismay of his friends, off he goes in the seemingly opposite direction, which eventually takes him perfectly to the right place, at exactly the right time to obtain exactly what he wants, with ease. The best part is that he follows his heart and intuition with absolute confidence and belief, not knowing why or what the outcome will be.

Ann: It made no logical sense, but he still did it.

Lamgan: This is a good example of the kind of path you must follow, and this is how you all begin to elevate your frequency to perfectly match this new heart frequency, new dimension, new world, new way of being. Many things will happen around you, as the Earth is changing too. So is your solar system, and you may think that it doesn't matter to you as a person what the solar system does. It matters, but in the grand scheme of all things, it doesn't matter.

What matters is your awareness; *keeping up* and adapting to the changes in and around you – keeping up with the frequency alterations coming at the planet from deep space and your Sun, plus also being aware of them when they do come in. This means seeing how you feel every day, making a mental note if any strange symptoms or feelings arise, such as changes in your mood or energy, changes in the quality of the light, etc. Many times we have prompted you to get in your car and drive into Wiltshire, into the countryside. We would have wished to make ourselves known on several occasions but you have paid no attention to your inner voice, and found many reasons not to come.

Elaine: And I am very sorry to say that he is right. I did find excuses not to go, because I thought to myself (my logical mind again!) you must be mad! Why drive all the way to Wiltshire just to sit in the car late at night? Had I known what was waiting for me, I would have been there faster than lightning. I didn't trust my instincts and intuition.

Lamgan: When you are willing, and trust enough to follow those whims, and you don't think to yourself as you did: 'Oh my goodness, I won't be able to get up in the morning', or: 'Oh dear it's going to cost too much for petrol', or: 'I'm going to be sat in the dark in the middle of some field somewhere, thinking to myself that I must be an idiot'. When you allow those things to sway you, *your life has no adventure.* Your life has no adventure, and you are stopping the flow of the connection between you and us. If you don't step into that flow and let it happen, you do not then arrive at the door where we can meet, where our energies blend and creativity begins.

Elaine: I must admit I am now very embarrassed about that.

Ann: I think everyone can sympathise, having been there myself, too. So really he is saying, pay attention to the signs and act on what suddenly feels the right thing to do, even if you've got to interrupt doing something else.

Lamgan: Absolutely. Make it part of your daily life to ask your conscious mind to sit, take a back seat and be quiet. As you're working, planting, doing housework, dishes, or whatever, just become aware of all your ordinary five senses more as a starter: your sense of smell, touch, taste, hearing, and sight. Then, go one step further and reach out for the subtler and finer levels of all those senses, and you will find that stepping between two worlds, two realities, two dimensions becomes easier and easier, because *now is the time* in which to do it.

Now is the time, and although the next dimension has always been all around you, it's easier to feel and sense now than it ever was. And within those higher vibrations are millions of things and events you have never seen or experienced before. Elaine, you have been on the edge, or 'bridge between', before and you have dipped your toes into it, in and out, in and out. We know because we have been with you when you've seen things that were incredible to you.

For all humans on Earth, whilst you are waiting for your material structures (which have kept you rigidly fixed in things) to break down, why don't you allow yourselves a bit more freedom, and choose to step up in awareness? You can break out of the old patterns and be the ones who choose to be free of the old paradigm. If you are willing enough to reform old beliefs and step into this new reality, you can taste it, see it, know it, and then you can lead by example.

Elaine, we know how difficult it is for you to broadcast this to all your brothers and sisters and say: 'Look, look what I've seen', because you sometimes fear judgement by others. We remind you of the rule of removing judgement. It's not good, it's not bad, it just is – and that everything is as it should be. Be in the Now moment and remove your judgement. Then whatever others may say, it makes no difference to you. This is one of the principles of loving yourself enough to BE yourself. Elaine, all you can do is offer and give, and within that lays fulfilment and peace for you. When you have given to others, if they choose to accept, that's fine, or not accept – that's ok too. Either way, it makes no difference. An opportunity to learn will come in some other way.

But, to all other people I remind: *You all must be responsible for yourselves*. Other people may do what they may, but it's important for you to lead the way by example, to do the practice yourself. Like many things on your Earth, a saying goes: How can you be a midwife if you've never had a baby? How can you be a chef if you've never made a cake? You have to do it. You have to walk your talk.

Ann: I am just wondering, how we can teach children this? Is it just by them observing how adults live and behave, or can children be taught this in a way they can understand so that it would be a natural way for them?

Lamgan: There are various ways. One is to begin with your own children, your own family, and you with your children, Ann. They always will be your children, no matter how old they are. Continue to show by example to *their* immediate children within the family also. But also there are many other ways. Volunteer to go into schools giving talks; writing books, and distributing knowledge; giving all you know freely amongst your local community.

There are many ways, and as people watch, hear and listen to you, it starts a ripple effect. You alone cannot change the entire world, but you can change one small piece, and if you change that one small piece, all the generations that ensue from that one small piece will be changed. So we must each do in our own corner.

Elaine: He is pulling from my mind a childhood hymn I remember: 'Jesus bids us shine like a pure, clear light, like a little candle burning in the night. In this world of darkness, we must shine, you in your small corner, and I in mine'.

Lamgan: You don't have to feel that you need to go out and change the whole world. Not necessary. Begin in your own corner with your own neighbour, with your own friend, by your own example. You needn't say: 'Oh, you *must* do this'; it could be more: 'Look what I did and it was amazing. Why don't you try it?' If you put these words on the internet, or in a book, then those who pick it up will, and those who don't, won't. Everything is just the way it should be. But let that be as it is.

Again, you can hear the conscious logical mind saying: 'What's the *right* way to do it? How should I do it, and is this enough?' Tell your conscious mind to take a seat, sit quietly while you let it flow, and do not worry about the 'how' or 'why'. Have the intention that it should flow out like a river, and then let the energy take care of itself carried on your good intent, because you do not know how powerful you are.

You do not know how much one good intention – one perfect harmonious vibrational intention from the heart – can have more effect than a thousand hours of trying from the wrong place. In fact your friend, Eckhart Tolle, is a good example of that. When he had something which came from his heart that he wanted to share, it went all around the world, globally. So, be assured that all you do is just perfect in the way that you do it; and remind yourself to be a good example to others, and do not get into the habit of being cross with yourself. This is negative self-judgement. Being cross or self-criticising is just an old habit, a bit like your conscious mind having a tennis match with itself saying, I should do this or that. Then you might say: 'No, no, be quiet', or, 'Oh, I'm always doing this', or, 'Here I go again. I thought those thoughts before'.

So we say to you, whatever negative thought your conscious mind presents you with, just constantly remind it to take a back seat, and become aware of your higher senses and deeper conscious flow. And for that moment in the Now that is all you can do.

Ann: I think it would be a wonderful world if we could encourage people to believe in their true potential.

Lamgan: Yes – empowerment for all, knowing how and what you as humans can achieve is, in reality, limitless. Begin with yourself, as always. First, believe in our own personal potential. All you need, more than that, is the knowing (not thinking) of how to *manage* your limitlessness, and how to change the way you do things. Cultivating your ability to radically change your approach to things in personal life and the world around you is the way forward.

You see around you many, many examples of success, and, if you take note, most of the endeavours that have the most success have come from very small beginnings. For example, there may be someone who makes jam that all the local neighbours' love. The neighbours suggest that they sell it in the local shop, and so on, and in the end it can develop and grow into an empire of jam-making – *if that is what they desire*. The potential for anything in the flow is always coming from the heart. If it's a good resonance, and a good, pure, intentional thing, whether it's jam, a cure for cancer, or a project to save the rainforests, it makes no difference. When it comes from the heart with good intent, the arrow of achievement will find its mark if you maintain that flow and do not strive to make it happen from logic.

How can I say it more clearly? Life on Earth is not meant to be a struggle. The more you think: 'How can I market 5,000 pots of jam?' the more you will puzzle over it and stop the flow. Stop thinking from logic, and allow it to be. If your intent is that this jam is so good you would love everyone to have some, it will happen. Do you see what I mean?

Ann: Yes, a different attitude.

Lamgan: I am coming to you reflecting the position that you are in right now, within the structure of your society, and the way your part of the world is. You must also remember that different parts of the world function at different levels of understanding. For example, what could be a problem to you, may not present a problem for someone in another part of the world. What could be a need and necessity to you may not be a need or necessity for someone else. Really, the bottom line for everyone is to become *more fully aware*. Become more aware of the planet that you live on, and the energy that connects you all. In that wonderful film you watched, *Avatar* (yes, we were watching you) awareness of the life, the breath and the energy of the planet is *everything*, and knowing what to do in the Now moment…trusting your heart and your intuition.

Elaine: I am seeing a scene in my mind now (from *Avatar*) when the female is about to shoot the soldier who was lost in the forest, and the sacred seed landed on her arrow. She could have ignored that, killed the man and her people would have eventually all been wiped out.

Lamgan: But she paid attention to a sign. All her senses were tuned in to what she felt was the right thing to do. That is not a lesson that we give you, but more a *directive* for assisting your transition, and that will assist your ability to keep up and stay in tune with what is happening on your planet right now, and indeed to the whole solar system.

Your planet is changing its resonance, changing the composition of the air – the particles in the air that you breathe – everything is changing. So to become more aware of that is to ride on top of it. To be unaware of what's happening could create problems in the physical body, or we will say – what you *perceive* as problems. So, for example, if you perceive yourself to be tired, or needing to lie down when you don't normally lie down and rest, or you feel the need to stay up all night when you normally sleep, you could interpret that as insomnia or exhaustion due to some problem in your diet. You could perceive that as *many* things which would become a problem for the conscious mind to solve. We say to you: *Don't do that*. If you are aware of subtle changes throughout your system and the world around you, you may observe how those changes are affecting your body.

Be a *watcher* and not an *analyser*.

Elaine: I feel like the transmission is done, even though it was shorter than I thought it was going to be, but that's fine.

Lamgan: Thank you, and please practise the awareness I explained to you tonight, and we will discuss your experiences. Part of teaching is for us to talk over how you handled something and how it went. We desire to take the work we want to do here up to a much higher level for ease of transmission, and increased awareness will fine tune your 'engine', and you will see how much difference there is.

Ann and Elaine: Thank you.

***

CHAPTER 2

The Antarctic and our connectedness to the Planet

Ann and I have met for the second session, and Lamgan begins the evening with information on an interesting topic which is very current today, regarding discoveries of elements, metals, and possible artefacts and remains of a civilisation deep in the ice in Antarctica, at the South Pole.

Lamgan: The frozen Arctic regions of Earth which cover a proportion of your planet at the poles hold a hidden history of which you know not. Within the ice, at the deepest region of Antarctica, are more particles of gold than there are available to you from the rest of the Earth today. The reason I am telling you this is because there are so many *more* things there of great value which are also hidden from you on your Earth, and the example I have given with gold is just a small part of what I mean.

The Arctic ice – both at the north and south poles – contains many minerals, some of which, at the deepest levels, you have never encountered before. They were laid down many millennia ago from solar storms, and came as cosmic particles that fell to Earth when Earth was still forming. There are also many layers of minerals, salts and metals that have come from volcanic activity that were trapped in the ionosphere of your planet, and fell to Earth eventually as the climate began to change. As these particles fell and the skies cleared, naturally the temperature became suddenly colder, so they were frozen in layers of history deeper than you have ever explored before, as witness to the kind of event that you could find yourself experiencing in the future.

We hear you talking about volcanic activity and the consequences and effect that it may have upon your civilisation. You have only touched on a portion of the effect that it could have on your civilised world. But do not be in fear, because adjustments and adaptations can be made by the people affected, and you will learn to live with a changing world. Just as new land is formed when a volcano erupts and discharges into the sea, so climate change is affected and the world begins to adapt on a much larger scale.

We also hear you talking about human adaptation and preparation for a self-sustaining practice which we applaud very much, because the world will change and your way of proceeding and living must change also.

In truth, whilst some things become more complex, more futuristic and more powerful, your use of energy – the very energy that makes your being, that sustains you and can empower you – the use and adaptation of that energy will go hand in hand with the *simplification of life*.

In the same way that you forged forward with the industrial revolution and became master and slave to machinery – and that era rose and fell with the advent of new technology such as robotics and computers – so will there be an exponential rise in new technology and a fall in the need for labour.

With this will come the lifestyle that you so desire to live. One of more leisure, of more self-gratifying pleasure and happiness, as you learn to become one with nature and to respect what nature has to give. We believe that due to the forces of nature you all will begin to value and preserve that which you already have, much more.

So, when I say this – my meaning is, in the event there arises widespread devastation of land due to natural occurrence – you will then treasure the small piece of land close by that you own or that you can use, because you will appreciate what it is like to lose, and therefore take more pleasure in looking after that which you have *not* lost. This is as you were saying earlier – we heard your reflections on people always coming together in unified intention during times of war, struggle and strife – and we would say to you, as my son said to you before, when the Earth decides to give you a catastrophe, it will be greater than war, but will produce the greater part of man's humanity for his fellow man. And there will come a time when all weapons will be laid down in order that survival is maintained. There will be no time and no reason to fight.

We have attempted to instigate this change within mankind through frequency and vibration, but we will also say that through natural occurrences throughout the solar system and the *Galaxy*, changes are happening according to natural laws, so that one thing will assist the other in your evolutionary growth towards a more peaceful and sharing society. We have always seen this, but never really revealed what we saw; but rather encouraged a growth of spiritual awareness. A growth of the brotherhood and sisterhood of mankind, and a growth of tolerance for all things living and all things sentient – of which I have spoken to you about before – recognising that *everything* has its value. There is not *one thing* on any planet, anywhere, which does not have its place and its value. Energetically speaking, you know nothing of that which I am telling you now. When I think of the value of sand or rock, or salt in the desert, you may think of some benefit, but we speak of subtler energetic energy which holds benefits that you do not know of yet.

Coming back to the polar ice caps, there are many things there which have been hidden from you for millennia. In fact when they were first laid down there was no one to witness the value. But now, as things change on Earth, the value of things newly discovered will become apparent. And as my son told you before, there will also be elements within the sea water that have come from the melted ice. It will give up its treasure into the sea for you to discover, in order to help change the way you live. The manufacture of new polymers with new ways of construction – that will not require that you level great tracts of land and deprive the Earth of one of the best means to transfer carbon dioxide into oxygen.

Elaine: And before Lamgan leaves he gives me an image of many people standing in a circle with their hands clasped together, and he says:

Lamgan: This is a strong circle of energetic, like minds, and when each person metaphorically extends a hand and holds hands with the one next to him, and it becomes an *unbroken* circle, then the power is multiplied...on and on. The strength of this energy is multiplied exponentially by the 'linking of hands' and the joining of energy. Those hands don't need to stay linked, they can break and join, and break and join, but it symbolises that when people assist one another, things happen miraculously overnight – and that you should make that your vision. You should make that your logo – that of joining hands worldwide.

Not only does it strengthen the circle, but the energy that passes around from one through another will double exponentially. It can be the greatest strength that you can call upon. So, with that I give thanks that you have been here to listen this evening, and I would be very honoured and pleased if I may come again, because I have much information to give you on physics, biology and chemistry and some of the more interesting features of the world as you live upon it now – but do not know, and the world that can be – that you can create.

Thank you.

Ann: Thank you very much, and thank you for coming.

Elaine: Do you have anything to say now, Ann? – Because Lamgan is now standing back.

Ann: Yes, I can feel somebody arriving.

Spirit Guide: Greetings to you.

Elaine: Greetings also to you.

Spirit Guide: This message that you have been given is not just for you, but for all people of Earth. Passing on this information is what will help things to change. Doing and making things differently from the way they have been done before in the past, will also help things to change.

It is the practicality of life that is important. It is important for people to understand that they can no longer rely on outside structures or some other group to support them in the life that they wish to live. It's important to learn to do things for yourselves, and help others too. Teaching them how to repair, renew or create from scratch – or grow things that will sustain the local economy.

We are most concerned about the way the younger generations are not encouraged *on all levels* to create a life which can sustain them and their future generations, considering what is happening on the planet now. By that, I mean what some human beings are doing to negatively affect your planet.

Our earnest hope is that politicians and governments will start to see how they can call on their own people for help, *and* assist change themselves – to a self-sustaining, self-supporting, and self-educating way of life, in a way that has never been done before.

It may seem to people that there is a global crisis, and for some this is a new challenge to overcome. But, for many, it only produces fear, because there is the seeming threat that all that they once held dear will be taken away from them, and that their material, comfortable life may be lost. But a materialistic life is often empty or devoid of anything spiritual, and if life has nothing in it that is spiritual then it will decay. It will lose the very energy it needs to keep itself alive. To live a life based solely on materialism is a road going nowhere. Crises that occur in every country will have been created by materialism.

Money of itself is not a bad thing, but the way you generate it colours the way you live alongside that money. If you are generous – not only with money, but generous by giving help and kindness to others, and money is not even involved – you will find that people world-wide will begin educating themselves in ways that they could never learn from books – because you learn that you *all* have things you can share with everyone..

Everyone has a unique talent, and each one is different. These talents are going to be what will rescue people from the interminable circle of going nowhere that exists in this world today. The life that most people live consists of getting up in the morning, going to work, coming home at night, watching entertainment to take their minds off a job they hate – or is not their particular choice. Basically living a life that has very little joy or value, compared to the life they might choose if they thought or knew how they could create it.

It takes a brave man to be the entrepreneur, but if you have the will to change things, and, if you can, the responsibility to teach how change can happen, then I think people will be surprised that they may not necessarily have to do it all on their own. Last week you talked about being spontaneous. Spontaneity can open up pathways that cannot be seen any other way. So it can be, with a desire to change your life, that you can create the life that will enable you to use your talents.

Have no fear of the future; always know that anything can happen. That in itself will bring you all the help you need. It will open doors to dialogue with other people; and for yourself – communicate – tell people what your hopes and dreams are! Don't keep it to yourself. We all have dreams; even your galactic cousins have dreams. They belong to a wonderful system of sharing, and they know how this works. They know how keeping links to each other creates a whole universe of opportunities. They know that the rhythm of sharing and caring creates many more opportunities for all. Through these opportunities, society develops and becomes greater, more fulfilling, more caring and nurturing than anything you have yet to see on this Earth. *And yet it can happen here.* Society can take great leaps and go forward. All it needs is for one person to feel the inspiration, start the movement, allow it to develop, and then share it.

Use other people's talents to broaden the picture when you don't have all the answers or skills yourself. Bring in a whole community spirit of like-minded people, and even not so like-minded people; because once this starts to grow, even those who have not much knowledge will want to learn and join in. Through their desire to learn, they too, will discover their talents.

Right now, the Earth is trying to educate people. The upheavals and disasters that you are witnessing – they are all ongoing lessons to teach you how to relate to each other in a positive way. To support each other in adversity, and to understand what it would be like to be in another person's shoes. When you hear of any disaster now, more and more there's a feeling and a need to reach out and help. Even if it's only a kind and caring thought sent out as a prayer through the ethers to reach those who are suffering. That's a very positive way of learning, because you draw yourself away from your own little world, and extend yourself. You can be a greater person by reaching out to all your fellow brothers and sisters across the Earth. Global communication is good and it will go on getting better.

People tend to focus with negative emotions on the next event or natural disaster in life, because that's what humankind is programmed to do. Then there is no room to focus on the good that happens all the time, it gets forgotten. It's better to mentally link into what happens globally in a positive way. When there is a disaster, focus more on the goodness of the human spirit, and the hearts of those who are dealing with it.

The way the human spirit is developing now is so important to the Earth. You must work in tandem with the Earth and Nature. The Earth will hear the call and respond to the human spirit that wishes to live in peace and have a benevolent heart. If you could but realise how much your thoughts touch Nature and the Earth, colouring the way the soul of the Earth reacts, thinks, and does, then you would change in an instant.

We strive to educate people to have much more awareness of themselves, each other, and all things. You can't go to war or be destructive and expect the Earth not to redress the balance. It's all about energy and keeping the balance. If you have war on the surface of the Earth – then there is war underneath, only Earth doesn't call it that. She has an elemental and energetic response. We are dealing with high energy, and this is a powerful force you have forgotten about! It's now a wake-up call for humans to change your ways.

Sometimes I think about the people of the Earth. From the dimension where I exist, I see a great bubble of love here and there, and then I see a dark cloud. The love wants to spread, and cover the whole Earth. But people are so blinded by their fear; they hold everything so tight within themselves, afraid that if they loosen up something will go wrong in their life. Internally, they are afraid to speak up. Externally, they are afraid to step outside of the box they put themselves in, and allow themselves to change.

The message tonight is that you (the people of Earth) are at last beginning to realise your deep connection to this planet, and that you all have been brought here to understand how all of nature – yourselves included, as well as the planet – is but all one whole energy, one entity. Nature encompasses every single living thing, be it inanimate or animate. It is all still living, in the sense that it has energy, and because everything touches everything else within that energy field, all is one. We are all made from the same atoms and molecules – like a colony of ants; we are all the same on the face of the Earth.

You cannot separate out the energy of the physical human being from the energy field surrounding that human being, and that energy is part of something else much larger. It's a fluid energy that is constantly in motion, constantly affected by everything it touches and resonates with.

(Pause as Ann's guide steps aside for a moment.)

Ann: I think scientists are beginning to understand this at last, that the finer vibrations of matter travel in and out of our everyday lives, through us, around us, in the ground that we tread on. That energy passes through the clouds above our heads, and it is affected by the sun's rays, our thoughts, actions and intentions and our in-breath and out-breath. It is also affected by our physical movement across the land. Everything is intertwined in such a way that you could say the planet and everything on it is one being – one cosmic being. Every person on this entire planet is part of this cellular structure.

Spirit Guide: I see that there is such potential for all the different races to come together. To still be individual and have their unique qualities of culture, but you can all relate and respond as one, as human beings. But there are steps of progression by humans to be taken before this happens. Some will be difficult, but living and learning through them will be so worthwhile. A large amount of good is generated every day on this planet, and that good has to work hard to keep the balance – but it can be done.

This life that you lead now can be better. By 'better', I don't mean living in a bigger house, or having more money, but better in the way that life becomes more fulfilled, because you will feel that every moment of every day fits you like a glove. Instead of living a life you think *has* to be lived because you have no choice, you can choose a life that *wants* to be lived. There is a lot of freedom in that – freedom that can't be easily understood in this day and age, but will eventually come to pass, and the beginnings of change are now happening. So, from here, I look outward and all I see is peace and contentment, and that is what I send out to everybody's heart. Peace and contentment. Thank you for listening.

Elaine: Thank you very much for those wonderful words.

Lamgan has just agreed and says:

Lamgan: The whole creation of any new society must come from the wishes of the heart, and those wishes from the heart can only come with love. When they come from your heart, then they are based in love, brotherhood, and in community sharing. But most important is equal love for fellow man, and love and respect for the self. The creation of this new way of living begins with the things that we have advised you to do today, and that is to dream, wish and flow with what is in your heart – Absolutely.

Elaine: And from that can come something wonderful for me, and I in turn can be an example as something others can aspire to. As we saw in the magazines that we were looking at earlier, when someone else begins to live the life that their heart says they want, that is a shining example for me to follow, and then others may follow my example if they wish. Energy of the heart is the strongest resonance of all.

Lamgan: Yes, and that's how it works. It starts with each individual person, and it grows. You will find that if you do this, you will meet people who feel the same, and have the same desire – maybe a slightly different vision – but you can collaborate with other people when your heart-mind is operating, rather than your brain. The new education is to encourage people to work with their heart more.

At some point later on another evening, because it is too big a subject, I would like someone to come through you perhaps – Elaine or Ann, to talk about the education of children. This is of *paramount* importance to the changes to come. They are the foundation stones – your young generations. They have to be allowed to learn the things that are much more important than academic knowledge. Academic knowledge is all well and good because it is interesting, but it won't build a self-sustaining life for a community in the changed world.

Elaine: To add to that, I am also feeling we must be like pebbles dropped in a pool, and begin with our own family; our own children, grandchildren, then neighbours and friends; or offer services to a school. But always begin with those closest to you – that's how things spread like ripples in a pool.

Lamgan: Yes, I totally agree with that. That is something that can be done without any problems. So we shall see what we shall see. I really thank you for listening and sitting so quietly. Thank you for the beautiful candle that you brought here last week. It is a wonderful soft light. I think the message I would like to give to most people at this point in time, is that everyone has the skills to create the life they would really love. The *courage* to do it is another thing, but they don't have to do it on their own.

Elaine: I understand that. Thank you!

Lamgan: And with that I will say goodnight.

***

CHAPTER 3

The Domed Cities of the Future: New Building Materials

Elaine: I am going to jump right in, just for a second, because before I'd even had a chance to really tune in, Lamgan, my Andromedan friend (who is the father of Pteplec), has just come in and is showing me the middle three fingers of his hand. And a question came up in my mind as to how many fingers they actually did have, because I've never thought about it, or looked before.

He now shows me his hand, which is very long, and very slender with a slight blue tinge to it. From the littlest finger – I see he has four fingers and a thumb – the fingers form a beautiful angle, like one half of a triangle, which means that his index finger is the longest finger of all. They gradually decrease in size as they go down from index finger to the littlest finger.

Ann: So quite different from ours?

Elaine: Oh yes, and when he holds out his hand like that, it forms a most beautiful shape.

Lamgan: That's all well and good, but that is not what is important. The three fingers that I show you represent what we will focus on tonight.

Elaine: What is it about the three fingers that is so important?

Lamgan: The three fingers represent three elements: three elements that make up a complete whole. They are the three elements of: gold, titanium, and....

Elaine: My mind then jumped to the logical next step which I thought was silver. I asked: Silver or Silver alloy? (And I don't think this is correct.)

Lamgan: This is not correct.

Elaine: He speaks about another element and it sounds and looks like the word Nibirium or Niobium. I've never heard of Nibirium, and perhaps it's a new element on the periodic table – I don't know. Or maybe I've got the spelling or the sense of it wrong, but the information about the three elements is what is important. I have a feeling that this third element (and we'll call it Niobium just for now), could potentially be incredibly strong and versatile when combined with the others. Stronger than anything we know of, and when it's blended with titanium and gold, it can become very flexible, so the end result would be very flexible strength.

Ann: What is it used for?

Lamgan: Titanium is what you call a self-healing metal. Titanium can be employed under circumstances where most other structural material would be subject to severe corrosion due to the properties of its oxide. It is highly resistant, and forms a self-healing coating about 0.01 mm thick. If the coating is damaged and the environment contains oxygen in some form, the titanium and oxygen react together and rebuild the oxide. The gold is there to make it malleable but it only needs to be present in trace amounts.

Elaine: He shows me that the Niobium, when mixed with the other elements in this new state, appears to be jet black, as if it is almost like volcanic glass, but it's not glass at all – it's a kind of soft sparkly black coloured material.

Ann: Like Obsidian?

Elaine: Not really, not quite as shiny, more of a dense but sparkly black, and of course the titanium is silvery coloured, and the gold is gold, etc. He is telling me that a mix of these three elements in certain proportions will make this new compound. They are not by any means in equal proportions.

Lamgan: No, you do not understand this correctly.

Elaine: I have the feeling from him, without any *major accuracy* at the moment; it would be a good proportion of the Niobium, perhaps eight-tenths, one-and-a-half-tenths titanium and half-a-tenth gold. This is the kind of ratio Lamgan is saying is needed to make this very, very strong but flexible material. The image I can see right now is of it coming out of a machine like a sausage, as a long solid cable. He says that the long cylindrical sausage of 'stuff' can be rolled, pressed, beaten; and what enables you to do that easily, is working with it at a certain specific temperature.

Once it cools and reaches normal temperature, then it becomes extremely strong, but still flexible. When I say flexible, it would be like a 'smart' building material. It would be earthquake-proof, but would remain in its shape and could bend or move in all kinds of directions. If it was hit with a sonic wave or an earthquake it would remain intact. He gives me an example:

Lamgan: Please imagine it was used to make a block of apartments. It would retain its shape provided that the foundations were made of the same material. Of course if you put it on concrete then the concrete is likely to crack under any stress; but it would not be appropriate to do that.

Elaine: He is now showing me strange-looking buildings on stilts, made of this composite sparkly material, and they're domed – not high like a half sphere – but more like an egg looks in a frying pan. The buildings are constructed as a dome with a flat bottom, on five legs (not four), and they can be built as a layered block of apartments forming the dome shape.

Ann: Like tiers?

Elaine: Yes, like a multi-layered cake.

Lamgan: Each dome is a multi-level living area. It can contain maybe a thousand living places all the way around, with a central garden. It is also tiered inside, so there are different levels.

Ann: So is this big, like a city?

Elaine: Yes, this is big, very big. It could be like a small city or a township, and very safe and secure. He is saying that you can use the legs that it stands on for entry, and they will be hollow inside, like lift shafts, because it is such a very strong material.

Ann: Is this a description of dwellings he is familiar with, perhaps where he lives?

Elaine: No, I think he's referring to something in our future. I remember that his son Pteplec did say to me, before, that we will find a new polymer in the future, and that we could make things that were both very strong and flexible. He said that we could build houses out of them, put pole-like structures into the ground to support them, and that there was an element found in sea water that was part of the equation for this polymer.

(Author's note: See: *To Andromeda and Beyond*, Elaine Thompson, 2008.)

Do you remember in last week's session that he previously talked about how much gold there was in the sea and under the ice? Perhaps he is just pulling that together now with this information about ample amounts of gold in seawater. This is me guessing now. I'm just trying to put things together.

Ann: Is the Nibirium/Niobium here, on Earth?

 Elaine: Apparently, yes. If it *is* Niobium, then it is already in use for many things. The interesting thing about the domes (which are made of this compound material but very, very thin) is that they look in some lights like sunglasses do when they go dark, and they also sparkle with thousands of different colours because of the titanium, so the surface reflects the light. They are very pretty, and not at all unpleasant. From a distance they look black but when you get closer to them they change, and when you're actually inside them it's like looking through tinted glass.

Ann: What sort of energy is being used in these domes?

Elaine: I'm pretty sure it's solar energy. Lamgan is now showing me that the domes can be constructed on different levels of ground. The legs of the domes can be interconnected with walkways, and when the domes open up at the top, they look almost like fractals or spirals from above. And each one of them connects, to spiral with another, so a group of them are really one huge, beautiful sculpture on the landscape, almost like platforms high in the sky. Not so tall as to be crazy high, but because they are so vast, there has to be really good ground clearance to allow trees and vegetation underneath and around to grow.

Lamgan points out now that due to whatever this building material is that makes up the polymer, the light will pass through it. So, although it casts a shadow, ultraviolet light from the sun and all the things that plants need to grow, still passes through the building. This ensures that the plants and trees are healthy, and that anything underneath the dome can survive and grow. If you imagine the height of the tallest rainforest, you could be sitting a hundred feet above that rainforest on one of these big dome platforms, so everything could continue on down below, and there would be access up and down via the legs, in what I suppose would be futuristic elevators.

Ann: So people can leave these cities and move around?

Elaine: Oh yes. I am being shown that, and as well as the elevators that go up and down, there are also flight decks for air-powered vehicles. And I can also see big tubes being used as connectors, like you would have a tunnel with a railway going through at high speed, but all done using the principle of pushing air either down or backwards and forwards. You can even get to other countries using these! Can you remember those old-fashioned shops where they used to pull a metal pulley and it shot a capsule full of money somewhere, using pneumatic air power?

Ann: And it went whizzing along a cable?

Elaine: Yes, like that. But this construction I see is using all very natural organic energy. You realise that energy to push air can come from steam turbines that are powered by hydrogen produced from water, using radio waves to separate out the hydrogen for fuel. Or maybe they would use solar power from the sun, or even 'free' energy, and that kind of thing – or maybe something we have not discovered yet...I think this may be coming, but perhaps we have to go forward at a steady pace. And now Lamgan is taking me north, to colder climates, showing me domed platforms that are lower to the ground, and they are white and really sparkling.

Lamgan: There is a slightly different proportion in the mix of elements used here. The proportion of titanium increases in a colder climate so that brittleness, due to freezing, does not occur.

Elaine: So I am assuming that it would need to be more flexible in order to be compatible with the freezing temperatures.

Ann: What are these Arctic domes made of?

Elaine: The same stuff.

Ann: Even though they're white and translucent?

Elaine: Yes, just formulated in different proportions. He is taking me to Africa now, and he says:

Lamgan: As the climate changes for exceedingly hot areas, the formula is the same. It changes only when you get to places that are regularly well below freezing, such as the northern hemisphere and the very southern tip of Antarctica. This polymer (as he calls it), can be used interplanetary. You can use this construction material on other worlds, such as your Moon or Mars, because it's very light to transport. But, you have to do something extra to it. It is quite light and flexible, and within the different gravities of different worlds it is easier to manipulate and use.

Elaine: He says in order to build a structure that big without the conventional methods (as we would think of a building site), there is something that you do to it...or a form that it takes...and he's showing me now that it's almost like putting together pieces. Like *Lego?*

Lamgan: No, it's very light until you intervene with a process, and then it becomes very solid and heavy. First, you construct; then comes the second process.

Elaine: And he's declining to tell me exactly what that is just yet.

Lamgan: You have some research to do first, but nevertheless it is possible.

Elaine: My first question – when I thought about building things on other planets – is how, or where, would you get all that titanium and gold, and if there's no sea, water or vegetation up there, where would you get all the raw materials? How could you transport it, and how would you put it together? You would surely have to have something like a smelting factory. With hindsight, I can see how this is very naive of me to even ask this!

Lamgan smiles and is saying: It's not like that at all.

As I understand it from the thoughts and imagery he is sending me, there is obviously some kind of process that you expose it to. So I only have a small part of the picture – more the concept and the possibilities. The gist of it is, that you can feed the raw materials into one end of a machine (my interpretation of it), then all the elements go through this particular process, and come out of a tube shape (like a sausage machine!) at the end. This circular rod of material can then be rolled, and as long as it's a certain temperature it can be pressed, shaped and cut, or whatever you want to do with it. You then have to do something else to it which solidifies it, which then brings back the tensile strength.

I've got a strong feeling it has to do with exposing it to a certain frequency of sound that somehow locks the molecules together into this very light, but very strong and flexible material that will load-bear millions of tonnes. Hmmm! Now he's showing me a big apple pie with a big bite taken out, and he says, smiling:

Lamgan: There! Is that a sufficient bite to keep you amused and busy for a while?

Elaine: I will have to pass this information on to my friend who is both a scientist and chemist, and see what he says. Do you have anyone with you yet, Ann?

Ann: I haven't felt anybody yet. Perhaps we can sit quietly for a little while. I do get the feeling that the Andromedans are trying to introduce us to future methods of engineering without it having to involve industrialisation. What it feels like, is that there is no massive mining any more in the future. I am not quite sure how they would extract the ore, but certainly what I'm seeing is that the planet is nourished in a way that it is not nourished at the moment. It would be interesting to find out how they mine this Niobium.

To me, it's a wonderful picture of a harmonious way to live, which seems to reflect how people live on other planets. They've managed to get through this age of industrialisation whereas we still strip our planet of everything in order to have what we think we want for a decent life. And they are showing us that we can move beyond that – and actually create a wonderful, comfortable life without doing it the way we've being doing it for centuries. I feel very encouraged with that, and I like this idea of a domed building.

Elaine: And do you know what the most fabulous thing was, and he is showing it again to me now? The sheer size of these amazing tiered domes! And the best aspect is that the human habitation area is just a thin ring around the edge of the dome, and the rest inside is all green: trees, parks, fountains, water, everything...and the top opens up to allow birds, insects, bees and butterflies to come in. All manner of natural wildlife, and sunshine and maybe rain too!

Ann: It's not really like a biosphere, is it?, because the top of the dome opens up. But does it protect people from the elements? Is that because something has happened to the planet in the future?

Elaine: No, not like a biosphere at all! I can see everything, all around where these domes are, and it's all as green as green can be. It is almost like a kind of rainforest underneath them, but with trees and landscape suited to the latitude and position on Earth.

Ann: So, man's footprint is vastly less?

Elaine: *Vastly reduced* from what it is now, which has allowed the whole of nature to recover its balance.

Ann: And to take over the surface of the Earth?

Elaine: Yes, and I have a feeling that ways of exploring that future nature are totally different from how we do it today. I see people using things that look similar to jet-packs. It's not the same however; it's more like a flying apparatus using the power of compressed air or antigravity to be able to get from one place to another (short distances). Imagine if you and I decided we'd like to travel to Egypt tomorrow. We could probably pretty much arrive there within a few hours if we used one of those tube things I described earlier. And the interesting thing is that the whole world is *not* covered in them.

Ann: Are they underground?

Elaine: No, no, they're high up in the air, with travel transport links to get there. So once you got to Egypt you might, say, arrive in Cairo, or somewhere like that, and then you go down to ground level and travel from there. You can travel anywhere! Everything either hovers or it's a very fast, high-speed thing, so that nature is allowed to rebalance and re-grow. Everything just looks so green. It looks really fantastic!

Lamgan: I remind you, this is not some other planet, and this is your future.

Ann: It begs the question. What do people do to occupy themselves? Are they working?

Lamgan: Exploring, and working at what pleases them the most. Being creative...

Ann: And communal living of any kind?

Lamgan: No, individual and family living.

Ann: But on the outer edges of these domed cities?

Lamgan: It can be as you wish...and not everyone will want or need to do it. There are many kinds of shapes and sizes to the domes. There are some very large domes with maybe a thousand dwellings, or even ten thousand living spaces. Each home is spacious and similar to what you in the western world would call houses, but they are actually just large living spaces. There are also smaller ones, too.

Elaine: Remember I said to you that you could come from one of these huge domes and zoom across to Egypt and get off at possibly Cairo? There the domes could also be up off the ground, but smaller and more strategically placed, so that they would fit and blend with each other, being at all different levels, respecting the Earth.

They're not all dotted around like mushrooms, they flow gracefully and they're in groups. I see a big tract of land where there is another smaller group, but positioned in tiers, not one on top of the other. On a slope, there might be a curve, like the Golden Mean curve – a shell shape, where the dome on the top of the slope is the centre, and the other domes coil around in a curve down to the ground, so the last one would be, for example, fifty to a hundred feet off the ground.

Ann: That would be very good – so it's architecturally beautiful?

Elaine: Absolutely! There's beauty *everywhere* in the shapes and the way it's put together. Everything is curved, soft, and integrated. When you look at it from above, it's not just big pillars and domes everywhere; they're spread out and arranged in beautiful geometric shapes. It can be like a spiral, or could look like a different geometric shape from above. Everything I see is exceptionally pleasing and energetically lovely, if you know what I mean.

Ann: I wonder what has happened to the concrete jungles that we have now. Do they get recycled or dug up and dumped?

Elaine: I don't know. But I do see that in our future, concrete has just disappeared.

Ann: This could be a long way in the future, what you're seeing.

Elaine: It could be, and then again if you begin with small versions of this, it could work. The future seems to be coming at us all so fast now, with so many rapid changes, anything is possible. As people change and want a better life, they will get more accustomed to it, once the beauty and benefits are realised. For example, imagine you had ten people in one small dome, or even ten separate families in a larger one, each with their own private spaces. The area beneath the dome would be their communal garden where all is shared and all contribute something, even if it's not gardening. And maybe they have an interior garden too, which can be a growing space for smaller vegetables and salads and things like that.

Lamgan: The domes can also be used as greenhouses. As times change (this was received a few years ago, and this information seems to be happening right now!), and things like industry and finance disintegrate and are no longer needed, the need for big business collapses and the existing system breaks down, ready for change. Then people will no longer want to live in the same way. They will gradually want to move out of the cities, where there is no green, and go to somewhere that can sustain them both physically, energetically, and spiritually.

As old buildings become unused and start to decay, then those unused buildings – especially in intensively inhabited cities – can be levelled or dug up one by one, and then replanted or left for nature and wildlife to take over again. Then, as people gradually migrate out to live in different circumstances, it can all begin to happen. There will always be kind and caring people who will turn waste land into gardens, because you are all intrinsically lovers of nature and the Earth, and everyone has so much untapped creativity and innovation in them.

Elaine: I see this all as he shows me, and it doesn't seem as if it's *that* far away. And when I estimate 'that far', if I said fifty years to completion...that's not really a long time. Because, according to my information, major things will happen to make those changes begin to occur on Earth. My current information as of 2017 (instead of back in 2010) is that this is all about to happen now. In fact we are in the middle of the biggest transformation we have ever known on Earth.

As a precursor to using the domed futuristic designs, people will realise that they don't want to cover up the land or build hardly anything on the ground anymore, because we will all recognise that we are covering up the very soil that we need, in order to live a healthy life. Just coming to me from Lamgan now, is the fact that it will be instigated because of the introduction of Extraterrestrials to our planet, and they will ask us why we cover up our land, and why we don't build elevated houses in order that our Earth can recover its balance.

Ann: We do an awful lot of covering things up, both literally and figuratively, don't we? (Smiles)

Elaine: If we followed their advice, then that would give us as much land as we need to grow food. People would then be able to walk around on it, work on it, and be creative – and it would get rid of all the miles and miles of tarmac, concrete roads and flyovers that we still need for cars, not to mention inner city concrete jungles! I cannot wait for hover cars or vehicles you can just fly in – perhaps with some kind of airpower or anti gravity, as seen in the film 'The Fifth Element', where cars can fly across land or water.

Now Lamgan is taking me to the San Francisco Bay Bridge. I see that bits of the bridge are still there, on both ends. Perhaps the bridge breaks at some point in the future? It is red, isn't it, or orange? I can see one end of it has tipped and fallen into the water, and the middle section is entirely gone. I see futuristic cars or vehicles of some sort with no wheels, taking off into the air about half a mile from the bridge, and then flying across the water to get from one side to the other.

Ann: For me, it paints a picture of collaboration, where people work together with a shared ideal. A supportive life where all involved share responsibility, making any project or job much easier – where people don't have to do everything on their own, because there's a better awareness of the benefits of helping others – more than we have today. People are all involved, with a natural instinct to use their skills, not just for themselves but for the good of all, too.

Elaine: Everywhere I looked within that whole scenario Lamgan showed me, I saw that everybody was very peaceable and friendly, with a unity of desire to live in harmony. I felt real waves of very positive energy, which resonated with community and co-operation. Within this, every person retained their uniqueness and individuality, whilst still being part of the whole.

Ann: I don't see a use for money within this system. The energy would be free energy, do you think?

Elaine: Yes, absolutely. It's all about using as much as you need or want, and the rest is shared.

Ann: In this new paradigm, there's no sense of having to hoard anything. There's always sufficient to go around. You know, I think it has been like that on Earth before, a long, long time ago. So perhaps our galactic cousins are just leading us back to something that they know has worked before? A society which can be about supporting each other, as well as self-supporting – it does paint a rather lovely picture, doesn't it?

Elaine: Lamgan has just added another thing, which I feel is very important.

Lamgan: When it comes to other concerns, such as the value of science, literature, art and such things like that – those things are not lost to you in the future. There will still be gatherings all over the world in such places as University campuses and science buildings, but all places of knowledge and learning will be in a very different format to what you have now. It will be one where everyone –across the world – collaborates and works together, as much of your science and physics needs to be revised, and you will have help to do this. People will work together with Extraterrestrial friends in order to understand, and re-understand science and physics, learning the truth about what larger science and mathematical principles really are.

Elaine: I think, Ann, when our Extraterrestrial brothers and sisters do eventually *really* arrive properly to teach us, that it will quickly make the biggest dynamic change the world has ever known. And I think there will be countries quicker than America, who will be beating down the door and saying: 'Yes, please, come and show us. We come in peace; we just want to learn from you, we trust you'. Everyone knows that if they'd wanted to 'shoot' us they would have done so by now. I mean, they've been here for thousands of years in one way or the other.

Lamgan: There are many, many ways to take over the population of any planet, and none of them include by force. There are other ways that you know not of that could be used by some if they wished to do so. This is not our wish, but you have *no idea* of the complexities of mind and energy control. We need no weapons.

Ann: That's a reassurance, and also very reassuring that that is not their intention at all. Our concept of what we think poses a threat is sometimes, I think, very, very naive. Some people do have a tendency to want to control and dominate everything on this planet in every possible way. Controlling people's lives has been the ethos of the few on Earth for a long time. It's promoted to us, that this is how you get on in the world – you take charge, be in control of others. But the Andromedans are showing you a very different outlook.

Elaine: It's completely radical when you think of it, compared with how we live now, where fear is created and nurtured so that everyone lives their life in stress and fear of what will come next – having been led into a life of little boxes – too afraid to even try to change themselves as they feel there is no point, and where survival seems to be the driving force.

But listen closely; we are now waking up, realising the power of collective consciousness and claiming our place in the wider cosmos, allowing ourselves to be the wonderful human beings that we have always been inside.

We think we all have to abide by the rules, but they are only rules set down by other human beings. So I feel, actually, that our Extraterrestrial friends from all over the universe are here now to help and guide us because, and only because, we are ready. People have been taught to believe in lack – that there's not enough. Not enough time, money, water, food, and land. We have been programmed to follow and do as we are told in a world created by those who want full control. But at last we now begin to wake up, be aware, and choose to change.

Ann: And everything has been put there, programmed into us to encourage that feeling of lack, especially when you think about mortgages and bank accounts.

Elaine: But then look at how we've learnt. I'm just seeing images of World War Two, when there was a lot of lack: lack of food, lack of resources, and yet we were – apart from the sadness and futile waste of life on all sides – pulled together by adversity, we ate healthier than we do today, and had more community spirit.

Ann: And we got through it alright didn't we? It was difficult. People got together, and helped each other, no matter who they were.

Elaine: If we develop that mind set again now (without the threat of war), encouraging equal selflessness, giving and sharing, we will turn the energy of everything around for the better, by knowing that when you need something it will always be available, so what would there be to worry about?

The big reminder here is that *we* are the ones that create our reality. Our combined consciousness is the biggest asset we have. If we always remember that doing to others as you would have done to yourself is the only way to live, together we can create a different world – a place of both individuality and unity, of each of us doing and sharing what we do best. We all have a gift or a talent, and so everyone has the same value as the next but in their own unique way. What a fabulous world!

Ann: It's going to take quite a few big steps for us to get there. Everybody's got to feel the same about it and be willing to be responsible for bringing that about.

Lamgan: With the arrival of different species and peoples from other planets, that alone is enough to gain everyone's attention.

Ann: Yes, and it's going to be very interesting!

Lamgan: It will not be at a time when the media can create lies. In other words there has to be a breakdown of...

Ann: ...communication?

Lamgan: Of the people and systems that control your world-wide media and newspapers. Those who tell you what news you are going to read today, and put it in such way as to promote control and fear. For example, today your media were saying: 'Is this the end of the European currency? Is the Euro about to crash and go down the drain?' Disaster, disaster – well, what does that actually mean?

Ann: It causes panic.

Lamgan: It causes panic amongst some people. And there is still the same number of coins in people's hands, still the same number of Euros in the bank, because it's all about promoting fear in order to manipulate your minds and your currency market. There has to be an event on Earth, and it is all in progress and happening now, when all your big, controlling institutions will lose their power. Then, when honesty can be spoken on every street corner, you will then see us in full force. So there will be no lies, no pretence – and no more creation of fear.

Elaine: I apologise now for taking over the conversation again, but I can now sense a very high vibrational presence coming in with you, Ann. It feels like a very fine vibration, almost Angelic.

Ann: I can feel something too. Yes, it is an interplanetary being, a wise one from another planet. Whether that's Angelic or not, I'm not sure. I think we've been sending out a signal and somehow what we have been talking about has been picked up.

Something is happening on Earth at the moment, a gathering of higher beings that are responsible for the protection of Earth. They're collaborating, and coming together because we are drawing nearer to a point in time that is pivotal to our future. And this high vibrational being is coming in along with someone else from another planetary realm to join with their brothers on the Earth. I will see if I can get closer to match the energy.

Higher Vibrational beings Speak through Ann: There is much cosmic energy flowing into the Earth at this time, and many other forms of energy that are helping both the planet and also the people on this Earth. A gathering of great beings have arrived, and they bring with them their highest energy in order to stabilise what is happening – and is about to happen – in the future.

(Author's note: As I look back, could these high vibrational beings be those from the 'Sphere Being Alliance'?)

There is much disturbance in many corners of the Earth, and this balance we bring is essential. Many wise men and women live here on the Earth, either reclusively or out amongst you in the general population – keeping their hearts very pure and clear, and their thoughts of a positive nature; helping to dispel hate and fear. For nothing can change unless this hate and fear is done away with, otherwise the people of the Earth will go on and on, continuously on this treadmill, rewriting history, turning the pages, saying the same thing, and repeating mistakes over and over again.

This is an important time for change and for people to be courageous about it; a time when people of the Earth must stop complaining, and instead look to ways that they can rebuild a better future for their children. Yes, there will have to come a time when people must work together, not for any personal gain, but to help each other, and out of that combined effort things will improve exponentially in ways that at the moment you can not realise. Because people on Earth are not yet ready at this moment (2010) – not ready to share, not ready to work together – just not ready.

But with the help of my brothers and sisters, and through the energies that we can control – which is the radiation from the cosmic sun that pours a vibrational energy into the planetary atmosphere and through it into the Earth – we will revitalise all and give more impetus for good. The power of love will come through, and that will help to dispel hate, despair and fear.

We ask you to believe this, for in the believing, it strengthens our purpose. It strengthens that which we aim to give. There will be a great healing but people must want it, must desire it. So the message we wish to give to all peoples of the Earth is as you have already said tonight: To live with no fear and no thought of personal gain, if that gain should take something away from somebody else that is in need. There must be more sharing, more caring, more giving. We will continue on many, many times, seasons, years, decades, to pour loving and balancing energy into this Earth.

This is a vitally important time not just for planet Earth, but for all of this part of the Galaxy that you live in. You are coming to a point where you will enter a stage that you have not been in before for countless, countless aeons. A stage where mystery, magic, spirituality and cosmic awareness, can all come together and create a new world, a new Earth, a new way of living.

All we ask is that you keep within your heart an open mind – which has nothing to do with the brain – and a deep knowing within you that all is working out in a good way, and that you need not have any worries or anxieties. Hold each day as it comes, spontaneously, doing those things which feel right for you to do. Choose a life that you would prefer to live, rather than a life that you are forced to live.

We come from far away, and we *will not leave* until our task is done and this Earth once again becomes a paradise. A place that you can truly say is your home, a place of joy, where you can live a fruitful life, not only of pleasure but of labour – labour where you love what you do – and you will all live in harmony and peace.

This may seem a tall order when you look at your life as it is now, but it will truly happen if you wish it. We know that most people on this Earth want to have a better life that is more joyful, more filled with contentment, and more gratifying than the life you have now. Perhaps it may take many generations or perhaps not, but you have to start somewhere, and it takes effort on your part; effort to make the determination to change your thought patterns, to live with a mind that sees *positivity* in everything, and that makes *no* judgement about anything; a mind that accepts the order of things that will follow in accordance with your actions.

Actions, that is a big word – because it creates a huge expanse of circumstances that are actually not just your actions, but everyone's actions, carving out a whole range of scenarios. So think before you act, but act so that you know what you are doing and where your thoughts are leading you. Being mindful is also very important. Mindful of the things you *think*, you *say*, you *do*, and the reactions that come about through all of those things.

We are doing our utmost at present to reach into the hearts of those who rule in the countries of the world. We reach into their hearts to help them recognise the things they do that are harmful to others, and we encourage them to give a nurturing energy to their people. This is indeed a very powerful process. Thought is a powerful medium. The Creator allows this to be done only at the hands of those who have the knowledge and wisdom to understand the results of what they do. And so we say you are being protected, but we cannot protect you *from yourselves*, so there is work for all of you to do. We can only encourage, plant a thought here and there, create an atmosphere of positive action, and, where necessary, positive impact. We can encourage people to pause and consider rather than to blindly plunge on, and to take time to really think.

The way you all live in this world has accelerated so much, that people are losing the ability to consider anything for more than a second. It is interesting to us that lately there has been a global surge of interest in poetry. Poetry is a language that allows you to become at-one with yourself and the world around you, and that is what we wish you to do more of. It gives you insight into feeling and to belonging. If mankind can feel he really belongs and is at one with nature, then maybe he will do something about improving the situation on this planet.

We encourage people to write poetry, to sing their song – and we know you have many good songs and many good singers. Sing a song to the Earth in your heart, and when it's done, know the Earth is calling back to you. Feel its essence, its sighing, as if saying a prayer of gratitude that humankind has at last recognised its potential to support each other worldwide. Earth is very willing to support life, all life. It will not tolerate war, nor tolerate destruction of any kind. Sing your own song to the Earth to give thanks for the life she supports you in. Thank you for allowing us to be here.

Elaine: Thank you, this was our pleasure. And I hope you will return to us some time in the future when we can meet again, so that we can hear further words of wisdom from you.

Higher Beings: We would like that. And maybe we will see what happens in the meantime.

After the session:

Ann: It's interesting how it happened that we both felt that same higher vibration strongly.

Elaine: Maybe that's an example of the spirit of sharing?

***

CHAPTER 4

The Future and the Past

Elaine: I feel moved to extend a very warm, open-hearted invitation to all of our Extraterrestrial friends, also those others of whom I feel are close to me, but unseen, and who reach me in moments of quietness with small signs, lights, and energy. A warm welcome from the heart because, from my point of view, I really, really wish that the day you enter into our lives – not just into our world or into our atmosphere but into our lives as an entire planet – I wish that day closer and closer, and I think you know that the majority of people here on Earth who know of your presence will welcome you with love and be eager for change. Thank you.

I have a very short message from one of my guides who is an Extraterrestrial with an elongated skull. I call her the "Light Being" as she always radiates so much light it's hard to see her sometimes! She says:

Light Being: You are so very fragile, you beings of Earth with your open hearts and closed minds. You that walk the streets of the cities who have lost the threads that connect you to the Earth and to the sky, who are caught in a web of illusion and deafening silence when it comes to connecting to your higher selves and All That Is. There may be times to come when some cities will be no more, when some jobs will be no more, and when the façade of work will alter so radically that people will fulfil their dreams and earn their money or their barter from within their own homes, whether it be using the internet or more locally in close community – it matters not. But the structure of your daily working lives will undergo radical change. In the same way that the Industrial Revolution brought unthinkable change to the masses, so too will this change create a world and a lifestyle that is so different from the one you still live in now.

And remember, if you stay in touch with the Earth herself you will have a knowing, a feeling of rightness about things to come, and day by day you will be preparing for that without knowing that you are doing so, because it feels so right.

The Earth's energy field holds within it the blueprint of the consciousness of the people. Rest assured that the move within people towards peace and changes can collectively be felt in every person in every country, because the consciousness that you all share is essentially one consciousness. And so, many of you now are refusing war, are refusing lies; and so you are changing consciousness yourselves for the betterment of mankind. You will see many more anomalies in the sky, and unexpected events from within your solar system and your galaxy. These solar events will be arriving, some to pass by Earth, but more to enter Earth's atmosphere and to have lasting effects upon the Earth.

The Earth herself, as you know, is like a dog that shakes water from its fur in order that it feels refreshed, clean, and eager to run again; but that shaking will cause disruption beyond that which you could dream. So, in a metaphorical way, we ask you to hold on tight, stay close to the skin of the Earth, like the skin of the dog. Hold on tight and wait for the changes to subside and the new peace and balance which will follow.

Elaine: My Extraterrestrial guide, who was speaking then, has now completed.

Ann: I have a being with me now who wishes to speak. I think he has lived on the Earth before. He no longer needs to come back to the Earth, but he lived at a time when man first came down to this planet as an etheric being. He says:

Ann's Guide: Good evening, my daughter, and thank you for having me here.

Elaine: Good evening. You're very welcome.

Guide: I would like to speak tonight of the time of then, in the past, as well as the time of now, in the present.

When man first came to this planet he was more evolved than you are now, which is a sad tale when you think of it. But then he didn't have the dense physical body to contend with. Mankind then was of a lighter vehicle, bringing with them the thoughts and memories of a more harmonious life elsewhere. The harmonious life they wished to establish on the Earth was, to some extent, successful. They brought with them great understanding of how the planet was still forming, still becoming the world that we know today. They lived for a great time on your planet in a non physical form, not as solid matter, so therefore were untouched by the creatures that were very physical at that time.

In their energy form they were able to create wonderful places of habitation and of worship, but not worship as you know it today. Their worship was of being at-one with the power of creation – the source of energy that gave them life. It also gave them the reason for living. They were able to communicate with other beings on other planets very, very easily. Their transport systems were also of pure energy, enabling them to cross dimensions, and they were used to other visitors coming to the Earth. And then, according to your religious history, it is written of the fall of man, or a plunging into darkness, which came about for several different reasons. The planet was evolving and the etheric beings knew that their time would at some point in the future come to an end.

Creation is all about moving on – change, constant change – and these energy beings knew that another form of life, a physical human form of life, would be the perfect vehicle to inhabit the planet at a specific time. These beings had a great choice: they could remove themselves and go back from whence they came, because they all remembered through their traditions where their ancestors had originally come from. They lived *long* lives, and some of your ancient books talk of people living for thousands of years. These beings lived long because they were untouched by disease, or by the stresses that your physical body has to go through today.

Then the time came for these beings to leave or ascend. This was their right, because they had earned it through the work they had done here, as cosmic engineers. They had helped the creation of this planet and the natural kingdom of nature, and their purpose had been fulfilled.

However, there was a deadline for them to leave the planet. But some of them had become so in love with this planet and all that they had helped to create, that they chose to stay of their own free will. They chose to allow their beautiful etheric bodies to be drawn down into denser matter. The planet was undergoing another change as well, which was one of many that has eventually made the world you experience today. You talk about modern climate change – well, there have been really dramatic changes in the past, and all of them unavoidable.

And so gradually over time, those who chose to stay created a physical body that was more like the physical body you have now – and they forgot where they had come from. They were visited by their galactic brothers and sisters so that they would not completely lose the memory of their origins; but then, again over time, when these visits ceased, the memories became confused. Rituals came into being, traditions became warped, and yet, deep down in their psyche, the human beings they had become needed to remember – it's just that their memories were not clear.

So they built a memory that would mean something, that would sustain them in the days to come, and give them faith and belief in a reason for them being here. How many times have you heard the younger generations saying: 'I don't know why I'm here'? Because the world nowadays is difficult to understand and truly comprehend, as it is now so complex.

There seems no rhyme or reason for the way you live. Your physical bodies react to illness, disease and climate, and yet all of this has come about over millennia, aeons of time, as a very gradual process that has brought you deeper into dense matter. At one point in your history you were in an even denser form than you are now. Gradually, from about a few hundred years ago, the physical bodies of people on this Earth have been growing less dense. It is a painfully slow process because it also needs a growing spiritual awareness that understands not only physical form but the energetic spiritual form, and that the two must live in harmony. If they do not, then the physical form becomes dominant.

To both of you I say that, even in your lifetime, you have seen vast changes in people's perception of religion, faith, or any sort of belief system. There are so many now it is hard to number them all, but within them all there is at least one great truth which says that you are one part of a greater whole, and that you cannot exist without this greater whole. Whether you call it God or Spirit or Life-force, it doesn't matter – you still cannot exist without it.

There is hope amongst people in the spiritual realms as well as those out in your universe, which live, breathe and know how creation works. You are beginning to grow in your understanding at last. It is also commonly known that all systems need to go through different levels in order to reach their wonderful final goal.Planet Earth is no exception to the rule. Having started off as a wonderful creation with full of knowledge of itself, it was then plunged into a situation where the Earth no longer had the only word about how it was going to be changed or sustained. Throughout all of that, the planet Earth has been patient. The planet's soul voice has listened to what man would like to do with his life, and it saddens the soul of the planet, because it is a wish that could be fulfilled. The way the planet feels it, is that mankind wishes to destroy itself.

Now is the time when people will stop and think: 'Where is this all going? What is happening on the planet now?' This is more than a wake-up call: it's a loud bugle call. It's a reveille! Stir yourselves; stop thinking of just your individual selves. Consider yourself, in the way you need to keep body and soul together, but also think of yourself as one part of a great energetic whole, and that the whole includes everybody on this planet. But there must be no judgement, no negative thoughts that say: Oh well, we should have thrown *those* people off the planet because they're the ones that have caused the chaos.

There must be no judgement of what has gone before and no judgement of what is happening now, only clear-sightedness of what needs to be done next.

Listen to the people – the young, the old – and the *wise* people – who have seen so much that they know where all of this is going. Each generation has its wise ones, but so often they are given very little hearing. People nod their heads and say: 'Oh yes, I agree'. But do they do anything about it? No, because it would disrupt their programmed routine of life. Nobody likes change, or their routine disrupted to the point where they have to change the way they live, think, and act. They don't need to go out into the street and shout for all to hear that they want change for the better, but rather, they need to create the change and build the harmony – step by step within themselves – each person individually. That's the way that change comes about. You don't need to go on a protest march or have a big conference, there just needs to be a great welling-up of understanding in all people's consciousness. This can come through prayer, meditation, or even just talking with each other about how different people would like to live their lives, and how much you all would like to have a life free of stress, anxiety, and emotional pain. We, from our side of things, do our best to send positive thoughts down to the people of Earth. We try to impress on people's thoughts that if they lift their heads up and keep their eyes on a positive goal in their life, it will make a huge difference. Even if the goal is ever so small, such as: I'm going to wash the breakfast dishes before I leave the house this morning, so that when I come home tonight it's not sitting in the sink, making me feel sad that my life is like the dishes in the sink.

How much better to come home, see everything washed and dried and put away in the cupboards, and then you can think: Great – my life is clear and organised, in a way that leaves me free to just be in the moment without any anxiety. If people could stop self-accusation and judgement – my goodness – what a wonderful world this would become. People create and cause their own pain. There are so many things that can be done to change this! We know it can be done, and much is already happening. People are feeling the coming change, and it will be one for the better.

There are souls on this planet who have great spiritual strength, and they do wonderful work regardless of whether anyone sees or hears them. They go about their daily lives doing what they do, because that's what gives them joy and nourishes them in their deepest innermost soul. Most of the time, their lives will brush up against others and sow a seed with something they do that is kind or gentle. It may be noticed by someone else who will eventually pass it on, finding their life feels slightly better for it. They in turn will guide someone else, and these mirror reflections will go around the planet in no time at all. In giving those small acts of kindness, there sets a glow in the spirit and soul of man which can never be extinguished, and will always be there. We encourage everyone to believe and know that the dawn is breaking, and that very soon there will be the sunrise. So be prepared for it. Go about your daily lives knowing that things will get better – and by that I don't mean that they'll get easier, for everyone has to take personal responsibility and work for the change they want most dearly.

Ann: My guide has no more to say, except to bring you blessings, Elaine, from some higher beings who have known you since childhood. And they say they will send you help whenever you need it.

Elaine: Thank you.

***

CHAPTER 5

A Message from the Lyran

Elaine: I've opened the meeting tonight because I've become very aware of *all* my guides being around me in the room. When I invited my Extraterrestrial friends to come in, I was also surprised to see the Extraterrestrial who is a representative of his entire race, and he shows himself to me as one whose root race began as insectoidal beings. He has previously told me his history of origin. He now looks somewhat different to how they were, but nevertheless that is where the root race originated. I have called him a Lyran in the past, but I think names sometimes only serve to confuse, as I don't really know where he originally comes from.

He tells me that he has come here tonight to speak to me *personally*, because I have reached a crossroads in my life where there are choices to be made. Clear decisions are in order as to which path I must follow, and they need to be brought forward. He reminds me of my age, and also tells me that the time from now on will be filled with interesting and unusual events – with changes in my position (where I live) and perception of mind that I had not expected. And as that day draws closer and our connection to the Extraterrestrials grows stronger, there are some things which need to be prepared for; and allowed the time in which they can develop.

Lyran: We first came to you when you were younger than three years old. We have used you, with your permission, as an experiment in just how much we could stretch the mind without it breaking under the strain. I know that this is a very crude way in which to put it, but there has to be a certain genetic predisposition and disposition in personality in order that you become a candidate for our exploration into how far we can go.

So far, there has been a great deal of information implanted deep in your memory from several races other than ourselves. Some of this information has already come forward; a lot of it remains still within you. And we would like to prepare the way, in order that this information can come to light, especially at a time when it will be most needed and understood. Had it come to light at an earlier time, it would have been generally dismissed and be left lying on the shelf like a forgotten book in a library. So we say, even now, the time is not quite yet here for the knowledge you have inside you to be made public. But preparation needs to be put into place so you can have the opportunity, encouragement and the wherewithal with which to bring it forward. We have listened and understood your situation and, together with members of other Extraterrestrial races, we have consulted on what would be the best way forward for you.

We also recognise that there is a bridge which needs to be built more strongly between us and those that guide you on the Earth plane. These are in fact your spiritual guides, and there needs to be a further higher vibrational bridge between your guides and yourself. This is so that you can manoeuvre yourself into the optimum position to obtain all that you want and need to be of further use, both to us and to be of service to the planet (which was our main aim in the beginning).

We chose you as an experiment in order that we could be involved when the Earth underwent changes, but also that we could be involved *practically* by offering advice and recommendations to any people of Earth that would listen. We are not seen as often as some of the more 'popular' Extraterrestrial races that contact people on Earth, but nevertheless we are here. And we stand back and away so that we can observe the progress.

Like a few of our galactic brothers or friends, we are primarily interested in genetic improving, and helping races of people to understand where they have come from and what they can become in the future. And to this end we have seeded the world with many people who have the capacity to be visionary. Now we are drawing closer to the finale and to the crucial point in time when these voices must rise and be heard even more strongly around the world. You have the means to be heard around the world with your electronic communication and internet, and now it is time that we begin to put these things into place.

Elaine, you believe that you do not dream much, or at least we should say that you do not *remember* much of what you do dream. The time has come for you to begin to remember. This is because we have had many meetings and many explorations into different planes of existence with you – and shown you many different levels of understanding of physics and science as you know it on the Earth. This is one reason why the theory of quantum energy resonates so strongly with you. This is because you know that within it lies a much bigger truth than is known to many scientists on Earth today.

We understand your surprise at times when things come out of your mouth that even *you* didn't know you knew about. We have been watching and waiting for these things to emerge, and we understand that you need a platform from which to share these things, whether it be with electronic media, paper media or simply by voice. The time has come – if you will, and are willing – to make noise, and be heard.

We do not come so much to help you to know how to fix things which are already in place on Earth – things that you deem to be wrong or not good for the planet. We come more to show you how to do things differently in the future, to show you of future innovations that can be the inspiration for scientists and people who work with new technology, so that they will aspire to create.

Once people see an image of something that seems impossible now, there will always be someone who will attempt to solve the problem of: 'How do we make that thing happen? How do we figure out how it works?' Such is the nature of the human being, and it is one that we admire very much; like the industry of ants when they come together as a whole colony and find the answer to a problem somewhere in the group.

As you may know, and we have told you before, we originated with a collective mind and our mind is still collective now. Even though our body shape has vastly changed and our agenda is somewhat different, we still have collective mind. So, what one knows, all will know; and although you may not realise it, the same principle applies to people on Earth.

Each individual knows everything that everyone else knows, you just don't *know* that you know it; and only when given the space, opportunity and time in which to allow it to bubble up and become apparent in your awareness – only when there is enough quiet time – does this in fact occur.

Due to the structure and nature of your society as it has been built, you give yourselves so very little time to think deeply, contemplate and allow all that you know to come to the surface. So, we will ask you to make changes, to follow through with the things you have declared that you will do both for yourself and for the external projects that you intend to put into action. But also we would say that your new idea recently spoken of earlier this evening – of taking some time out just to think and to allow inspiration to guide you – is a very good idea indeed. And it will not take weeks, nor will it take days. Moments are more like all that you need to be inspired.

And now when I speak of this, I speak to Ann directly as well. Because today she has experienced a new thing – that when her mind is free of things to do and places to go, and allowed to gently unfold, the most wonderful things can happen. And if every day were like today, then she would begin to see that you all are living on an entirely different level of being; a level in which the most important thing is the Now, and that those things that are brought in from the past or the future only serve to cloud the present moment.

However, we do look to your future, Elaine, in bringing this message today. We give you the visual imagery of a crossroads to show you that your pathway does not involve a right or left turn, but continues on straight to the destiny that we have mapped out for you (with your agreement) as well. Metaphorically speaking this is a path which is very straight, uncomplicated, and very open and empty at the moment. This is because you need to sow all the seeds of metaphorical trees and flowers along the way, as you go. So, how your journey is experienced will be entirely down to the things that you allow to prosper, and the seeds that you sow. The most important thing to remember is that you can *really trust* that your path is straight as an arrow and leads you to the place you really want to go in your heart.

I can see that this is hidden from you right now. You know that there is something there in the future at the end of your lifetime, but as such you cannot see it. This is where the element of trust becomes most valuable. We would ask you to find a place that makes your heart sing and makes your soul peaceful, and not to give thought about: 'Who will be my clients?' or, 'What will I work at?', 'Which thing to do first?' and so on and so forth, which we have heard you talking about many times. But rather to find yourself and *allow* yourself to be vibrating at the right level and the right energy (you understand this). And you *know* that when you are making the right sound, all the things you need, all the things that are in harmony with you, will be attracted to you like a magnet.

We would ask you not to postpone too long, and you know you have a concept of the time period we are speaking of in your mind, in which to make a definite change. Be inspired by our presence here tonight. We do not come often, and when we do, we come with a purpose and a design that needs to be put in place and understood tonight. We encourage this change of vibration because we need to interact with you again.

And when we say this, you are to understand that we need closer contact with you once more in your life – as we did when you were very young, and as we have had periodically through your life. This will complete the full circle and then all that remains – and we will explain with another metaphor – is that when the circle is whole and complete, then it is time to set the diamond in the ring. And the diamond will be for you to give everything that you hold within you, openly and freely for others to listen to or to understand.

This will be *our* diamond also, because this project is one of many that we have instigated with you and many others across this planet. Now is the time to see all those other diamonds sparkle, now is the time to see them reflecting each other's light from a distance. So, if there are others in other countries, then it is time you found each other, and *by your light shall you be seen.* In fact, to all of you who came into this world at this special time with the gift of seeing and understanding – such as Ann – it is indeed time for you to shine your light and allow others to see it.

We began by telling you about remembering dreams. We will again come full circle and remind you again that the things you may see and remember from your dreams will be the impetus that pushes you more strongly towards your goal. We know what you are thinking: you are thinking that you never remember your dreams. All through your life you have had difficulty with remembering, but we ask you to remember this: there once was a time – and you speak about it very often – when you had a very vivid dream during the day and remembered it, precisely, and this was the beginning of your understanding that sound can heal all things. So having said that, we need not say more.

We ask you and Ann, that you take heart and find within you the peace and courage to step out on these new ventures, to walk all untrodden paths and *be* the spirit of adventure, because there will be much to see, experience and speak about over the next coming years. And if you can support one another in what you do, then you will find that two heads are better than one, and four hands are better than two.

So having said that, communication ends now, and just as we leave we give thanks to you for being there to receive our message this evening, and leave with an assurance that if you stay *aware* you will notice things leading you in the right direction on a daily basis, and awareness begins with being in the moment.

Goodbye.

Ann: Goodbye, and thank you.

***

CHAPTER 6

July 2010: The Galactic Nations gather to Discuss a Rogue Asteroid

Elaine: At the moment I'm going through the welcome procedure that brings in my guides and Extraterrestrial friends. I know that my guides are around, but I feel very different today, almost as if there is a detached part of me somewhere else. It feels like I'm not really on the same level, plain or dimension as them tonight. Whilst I was making contact, I was actually taken by my Extraterrestrial friends a long way out into space – to some unknown coordinate – and I saw in the distance a *really* big starship.

They guide me to the inside of the ship, and I can see that there is a gathering of Nations on this ship. There different planetary beings from everywhere, who might be part of the Galactic Federation – I don't know – and they are discussing Planet Earth. It seems that they are not too concerned with what's going on with Planet Earth *right now*, (2010) regarding natural disasters such as erupting volcanoes and earthquakes. The topic for discussion is that they are more concerned *with what is approaching us from space*. The telepathic image I'm being shown now is of an asteroid. But the important point is that it's a very large asteroid – and they are stressing that it's travelling very fast. I see it coming at me directly, and now they take me to an area of space very close to Jupiter.

I will describe what I'm seeing in my mind. I am being given a moving video image of an asteroid passing by, very close to Jupiter. The reason I see it this way, is because they want me to know just how big this is in relation to the size of Earth. So after comparing it to planetary sizes, I now realise that it appears to be much larger than Earth. I see its trajectory takes it between Jupiter and whatever the next planet along is (possibly Mars I would think), following an arc or curved pathway.

Now they show me that it passes so close to Jupiter that it bounces out of – or off of – its giant magnetic field. As I watch it, I see it passing Jupiter, and then it goes on to pass us on the side closest to Earth. It then enters an enormous curved swing in an arc shape. They tell me that the effect of Jupiter's field is going to slingshot it around and send it past Earth. I see Earth now, and it will pass in the distance across the orbital path of Earth as it travels through space, curve back around behind the Earth, and then fly back towards the Sun. I am told that there is not really a worry about it impacting Earth, as apparently it's too big!

I am also informed that it's actually being controlled by something that comes from deep space, and will come under the effect of the gravitational pull of the Sun – as we are on Earth. It's much too big to hold an orbit around Earth, and it reminds me of one of those metal ball bearings inside of a pinball machine. So it will shoot towards Earth after going past Jupiter, and back round the other way.

And the really big point they're making about this, is concerning which elements it will affect on Earth. They show me the tides, the water in the oceans and lakes, the overall water tables on Earth and the weather. It's exerting an enormously huge drag effect, similar to when we get a mega full moon that creates a huge pull on the tides. It will be like that but much, much bigger.

I have now been taken back to outside the spaceship where I began, and I'm still looking at the asteroid from my position there, and I see it's still a long way away. I am outside of the ship because they want me to really look into deep space beyond and towards the asteroid, to see how fast it's coming, and to point out how far away it actually is, (in 2010). I don't know whether I'm getting this right, but it feels like it's a couple of light years away (not that I know what light years are, or how far that it is).

(Author's note: I have now researched that this is about 12 trillion miles, and I have tried to calculate its time of arrival, but as I don't know the speed or mass of the asteroid, it's not working!)

I'm a little more than concerned as it seems to be travelling extremely fast! But I'm sure NASA and our astronomers will surely be aware of it well in advance. They will no doubt detect and calculate the speed as it travels, and be able to predict its pathway across space towards Jupiter as opposed to heading directly towards Earth. I feel though, that the slingshot effect of it curving around Jupiter is going to be a bit of a surprise.

Ann: So it could cause all sorts of problems?

Elaine: Yes, it could cause huge problems for Earth with the oceans, weather and water in general. They are saying that it's going to be travelling at such a velocity of speed past Earth, that it won't be affected by Earth's gravity, as our gravity is obviously not as strong as the Sun's, but it *will* return past Earth, attracted by the Sun. So I'm asking them now – if it is being controlled by the Sun's gravity and other things – why is it heading this way anyway, and what actually is it?

So they show me again, and as I'm seeing it go past Jupiter, I am very surprised to see that it's quite big in comparison to Jupiter. I know Jupiter is *huge* compared to Earth, and I can see for myself that this asteroid is as big as the Earth or even bigger.

Ann: Really?

Elaine: Yes, because if you compare Earth in to Jupiter, Earth is tiny like the size of a pea. So if we had something that big passing by us – that close – I wonder? I don't suppose, (and this is my speculation now), that this could be related to what everyone has called the mysterious 12th planet? Because my thought was, is it actually an asteroid or misshapen 'planet' that's in a mega large orbit around the Sun? Or is it just a random asteroid that has come from somewhere else – maybe from a planetary explosion or something? – And the Extraterrestrials are not actually giving me an answer on that.

Ann: Can you see it at all?

Elaine: Yes, it's just like an enormous body of rock in the shape of a big knobbly potato!

Ann: So it's not round?

Elaine: No, it's not a round planet shape at all. I see it clearly, and it looks like a misshapen rock of gargantuan proportions. So I speculate that part of an extremely large planet (larger than any in our solar system) has broken away or something like that – or maybe it has been orbiting a larger planet in space and somehow been flung away out into space? Now I have just asked them the question, should I be worried? And I just got a very visual image of me standing in oil skins, a sou'wester (a waterproof hat with a broad flap covering the neck) and carrying a big umbrella – (that's their sense of humour) – and they are saying that if you're anywhere near the coast you're going to get very, very wet, and equally so anywhere else in the world. Because it will not just be tidal reaction, it will be rain as well and everything else that goes with such an event. But they also say it will only last a couple of days.

Ann: And will things go back to normal?

Elaine: Um, yes, I think they will, but there will still be a tremendous amount of damage everywhere. When you think about all the coastlines there are all around the world, that kind of tidal extreme could be monumental. I also get the feeling that it's going to have more affect on America, and then Europe initially – that part of Earth.

Ann: So the Northern hemisphere?

Elaine: Yes, we will be facing it as it passes by. But then again, when water gets shifted on one side of the Earth, it has got to flow back in the other direction, so I assume it will have a huge effect all over the whole planet. Umm…I am just seeing a visual image now of when Atlantis sank. Oh dear, I hope they don't mean that huge things are going to happen like that on Earth!

Ann: Is there any way of diverting it? Have they thought of that?

Elaine: I'll ask.

They are saying that there is nothing that they have *right now* that is big enough or strong enough to make that much of an impact on it (which doesn't mean to say that there won't be in the future). If you think of something that is planet sized, you could hardly see spaceships pushing that out of the way! I don't think they have any kind of force field that's strong enough to do it, *here yet* – unless there is some kind of intervention from more advanced higher beings with mastery of matter. And I am sure that they are out there, maybe closer than we think!

(Author's note: I feel that the 'Sphere Alliance Beings' that are here right now could handle it, if needed!)

I don't think it's something that the Extraterrestrials I am talking to now are actually able do, because they now show me a holographic picture of our solar system from above. It's like the pictures you see in encyclopaedias, with the Sun in the middle, and the drawn circles that go around marking the orbits and positions of the planets. If you imagine the Sun in front of you, and that you've got Jupiter to your right on its orbit, Earth is closer to the Sun, positioned just a little bit off-centre to your left. The asteroid is arriving on the right side of the Sun, and then it's going to zoom past the Sun and cut between Jupiter and Earth. Then it will pass on the near side (to Earth) of Jupiter (as pictured on the visual solar system) and go further out in an arc – and then slingshot around past Earth, looping back toward the Sun.

If you haven't got this clearly yet, imagine your two hands in the air in front of you, with palms facing in – imagining that your right hand is Jupiter, your left hand is Earth, and the Sun is right in the centre of the room in front of you. It's going to come from the right of the Sun, and pass on the inside of Jupiter (on the palm side of your hand), curve around in line with your stomach area, then go forward on the palm side of your left hand, with the Earth on the other side (back of your hand), then straight back towards and pass into space to the left of the Sun.

It makes me think that it has a mega huge orbit, and on the far side of the Sun it does a great big loop way out of our solar system – but on the nearside of the Sun where we are in our local solar system, it has a very short loop.

Ann: It's closer?

Elaine: Yes, and it's only because its passing so close to Jupiter and the Sun's gravity, that it does such a sharp turn around again.

Ann: So has it been on this orbit before?

Elaine: Well, maybe it has. I really don't know anything about astronomy, so I cannot comment accurately on that, but it could be. As I see it, it's definitely *not* a round planet, but it's certainly planet sized, but a very different shape. So I'll just ask them if there's anything else. They show me now, that on that day, or on those days when it passes – that any star ships that are around Earth now will be well out of the way on the other side of the Earth – on the far side, for their own protection.

Ann: It might be very dramatic.

Elaine: Yes, they are saying that the gravitational pull of it is so strong; if you're not already locked in somewhere else (or have another planet as a shield) you could easily get caught up in its effect.

Ann: Goodness, let's hope it doesn't happen like that! That is pretty dramatic. Will astronomers here have any advance warning?

Elaine: Oh yes, they'll know its coming.

Ann: And they'll know how close it's going to be?

Elaine: Yes, but the thing I think that they may miss, is the fact that when it goes past a large planetary body like Jupiter; it will double back faster than they thought. We know it will slingshot around in an arc, and there may be some scientists or astronomers who will calculate the weight, size and mass, and realise that when it goes past Jupiter it is going to be flung in another direction.

Ann: Right! So do you think there will be some warning?

Elaine: Yes, I think there must be, but they may not realise quite the degree of effect it will have. I suppose it depends on how far from Earth it is, in space. And you know we've had comets and asteroids go past before and they don't usually affect tides and things like that.

I'm now going back to the interior of the spaceship, and I see quite a number of the tall-headed Extraterrestrials talking amongst themselves.

Ann: Is there any particular language that you can hear or is it just inaudible?

Elaine: That's an interesting question. I hear very tonal musical language and I can feel that they use telepathy for the big concept, and tonal language for the details. Another thing has just come up in their discussion, which is interesting – and that is that they know the Earth will survive. Apparently, this asteroid has come this way before, many thousands of years ago, hence the big orbit. But they are very much aware of the problems it will cause when it passes so close, as our planet is now much more densely populated.

Ann: So are they going to keep a watchful eye on us?

Elaine: Of course. I feel there are going to be further developments coming; they are just deciding what action to take, if any.

Because the population on Earth has grown so much with so many cities by the coast, I feel there is some debate amongst the delegates as to whether something major should be done. I think it's a question of shall we intervene and offer assistance – or should we (as we cannot stop it) offer assistance in a different way?

The options I feel are that they could pick people up and put them somewhere else very quickly – without people actually even realising what has happened. It would be as if you suddenly woke up and you were somewhere else – which again, they tell me – could also cause a huge amount of confusion. There is also an option to telepathically warn many people and help them to feel that they really have to move away from the coast, even if it's only temporarily for a couple of weeks. This option is so that lives will be saved, even though buildings may not. So the debate goes on amongst all of them as to what is the best approach. When you think about the whole of Earth – that's a pretty big job!

Ann: It's catastrophic, really, isn't it? I'm trying to imagine it – the devastation!

Elaine: Yes – and surely a huge amount of people to take care of as well. From what I can hear right now, the telepathic influence for people to get up and move option is coming out on top.

Ann: Animals will know when to move!

Elaine: Maybe there will be a call to evacuate the coastal areas as NASA, all governments and astronomers will see it weeks and weeks – if not months – before it comes too close.

Ann: So is this inevitable?

Elaine: Well… I assume so, but having said that, I am only repeating all that they have shown and told me, and what they are considering in this debate. They do remind me that there are many factors that can change events, and also that there are very many things in science and physics that we know nothing about on Earth as yet – so anything is possible.

And do you know what they are showing me now? When this asteroid passed Earth eons before, they show me that a small chunk of it broke off – or possibly part of its debris field – and was dragged into Earth's gravitational field. And my *speculation* is – that when that stray meteor did hit the Earth, it was probably when all the dinosaurs died.

So it must have been orbiting on this path for a very long time. But I feel strongly that apart from tiny fragments – in which case we would get lots of shooting stars – nothing huge like that will break off this time, because that really would be fatal for all of us – and I don't see that scenario at all. They say that if anything changes in a way that might be not so good for us, they will definitely help us with that.

Ann: Right, so are there any sunnier prospects to come?

Elaine: I have asked them why they are showing me this now, and they say: 'So that it can be broadcast in just one of many ways'. So I assume this information will be given to a lot of other people all around the world as well as us. Also they add that it's because we have a right to know, and because it will interfere on a huge scale with our electrical communications.

Ann: Yes, I was just thinking that might happen. So communications will falter?

Elaine: Yes. It will cause an Aurora Borealis everywhere, and everyone will be able to see it. That seems like an impossible thing to happen – with something that big, it just seems implausible. I'm only repeating what they are telling me, but to me it seems unbelievable that something that big could pass that close to Earth.

Ann: Yes, well we shall see.

(Author's note. I have learned a lot in the last few years, and I now know from further information given to me from them, that my understanding of what was being discussed by the delegates there was very simplistic).

Elaine: I don't quite understand the whole of this. My question to them was: 'Instead of moving any spaceships to the other side of the planet, why don't you change the vibrations of your ships and just slip into another dimension? Hmm, and as an answer to that, I am told that the shock waves or reverberation from this asteroid will pass through all the dimensions, because of the speed it's going at. Anything travelling through space which passes that close to any other planetary body – at any speed – makes a sound vibration, and the sound waves pass through everything, including dimensions. It's a bit like a sonic boom – it goes out through all dimensions and 'rattles all the windows' making ripples in time and space.

Ann: So it's really going to be awfully big and the effect very noticeable?

Elaine: I think it just might be!

Ann: What about the Moon? Will it affect the orbit of the Moon?

Elaine: Hmm... Now there's a very good question! In answer to that, they are showing me a visual. So – imagine that *you* are planet Earth, and that the asteroid is passing in front of you from right to left. The Moon will be – at the point of closest contact – somewhere in the vicinity of your left shoulder blade.

Ann: So as it passes, the Moon will be on the other side of Earth?

Elaine: Well, the Moon – as you know – orbits the Earth once a day. I'm told that at the most dangerous point in time, the Moon will be three quarters of the way around the Earth, and they do not say any more. I would have thought that as the Moon goes so fast around the Earth, and presuming the asteroid might take a couple of days at least to get past us, it's going to be inevitable that it will make an energetic impact on the Moon.

Ann: You would think so, wouldn't you, unless it is travelling super fast?

Elaine: I don't understand how the Moon cannot be affected, unless there's some kind of shield, force field, or gravitational thing that protects it. I don't know, but that's a really good question, Ann.

(Author's note: Please check out the existence of the LOC (Lunar Operations Command), and the 'Sphere Being Alliance' concerning the protective planet-sized spheres that the Blue Avians have placed throughout our solar system to protect us from cosmic waves – as talked about by Corey Goode, in 'Cosmic Disclosure' on Gaia.com)

Elaine: I am going to see if there is anything else they have to tell me. That's strange – I am now seeing a kind of structure. Visualise fence panels, but imagine them made out of bendy bamboo. I now see two fence panels joined together by a central pole, so that you could fold them back into a 'V' shape. I can see these V-shaped panels on beaches – and I am talking about enormous ones – the size and shape of the front of an aircraft carrier. The individual pieces of wood in the 'fence panel' can move backwards and forwards, so that they can act as a buffer against any incoming water, but they also are flexible. I see them letting the sea water flow through, because the V shapes are pointed *out* to sea. This would lessen the impact of any tidal water. Then when the water rushes back out to sea, the panels open out and all the water is strained through the gaps, and anything else is trapped behind the fence (at the shoreline). It's a bit like window louvres or slats on a window blind, but made of strong 'bamboo' type material that's very flexible, and bends.

Personally, I can't see how on earth that would work as a barrier. Just imagine if there were cars and houses being washed out to sea? It would surely just break everything down!

Ann: What are these structures made of?

Elaine: Well, it looked like bamboo but I think that's just my interpretation. It is really a flexible, very tough, light-coloured material, that clicks and clacks up and down, sounding like a bobbin on a loom. The slats are curved on both ends, a bit like the shape of an old Victorian nail buffer. The individual slats are very long extended oval shapes. All the pieces in this 'barrier' fence are that shape, and they all move backwards and forwards. When the water comes at them they are pushed inwards, but when the water flows back out they flap up and open, and the barrier acts like a strainer for large objects.

Ann: Is that to stop anything being washed out to sea?

Elaine: Maybe it's for saving people? I can't yet see how it could work effectively. But then, sometimes what you think are the simplest things, turn out to work really well.

Ann: So are these wedge-shaped structures joined close together?

Elaine: Yes. If you were drawing it on paper it would be like lots of

V shapes in a line on the beaches and all the coastlines.

Ann: And how tall are they?

Elaine: Taller than a house.

Ann: So would these structures be built on beaches prior to any flooding in order to stem the tide?

Elaine: Do you know Ann, I don't know. I have to get past myself in order to see how this could work. Who would supply it, how would it get built – *and* take on board what they are showing me as a method to minimise damage. My logical mind is saying, if the sea is coming in with that kind of force, nothing would stand up to it. But maybe they will let us know. I am not an expert, and there just may be someone out there in the world who knows about this method of minimising damage.

I'm now getting really hot here…I don't know what's going on. I'll be quiet for a moment and see what they say. I am becoming very aware of the clocks in the room, the church bells outside, and the rain. And because I let my logical mind interfere with the end of the session then, I have lost my deep contact. I don't know that I am going to receive any more, as I have now gone back to the spaceship, and all I can hear is a lot of white noise. I almost feel embarrassed, because I have told you what I was shown regarding defences against the sea, but my logical mind interfered with an opinion, and was saying – how impossible is that? But then again… what do I know? Anything is possible!

***

CHAPTER 7

Macro and Micro: The Birth of a Universe, and the Beginning of a New Age.

Elaine: So blessings to you here on this gathering this evening. I would like to thank *all* of my guides and the other beings who come to be with me this evening. I welcome and thank Ann's guides, and I extend a very warm and open heart to all our Extraterrestrial friends – including all those that we have known in the past, and those that maybe we shall meet in the future. I would like to invite the Angelic realms to preside over our meeting to lift the vibrations, so that all that we receive is of the highest vibration and the best quality.

Elaine: The first thing I would like to comment on, is the fact that my guides – who I can usually feel, sense and see in the room, are not 'in the room' this evening. I can only explain it as them being 'somewhere out there'. I feel that the family members who sometimes come with my guides are quite close, but the normal guides who generally come, are not here. It seems as if they are distant, and suddenly I'm now standing with them, somewhere in space, with a backdrop of stars and planets behind them! It appears as if they are standing on or in thin air, and I have no idea why.

Except that now I see a great light rushing in from deep space, and it feels like a person – a someone – or a some-thing. At the moment I can just see the light, and this light is stationary in the centre of the semicircle of my guides, and the light is now moving like flames would move. It's certainly a very spectacular light – and I have no idea who is in there, or what it is.

Ann: I'm just going to see if there's something coming through for me, as I feel something in my right ear.

Elaine: Ok.

Ann: There are beings that are coming to observe. The light that you saw, Elaine, is these beings. They are here because either they have not been in this part of the Galaxy or the Universe before, or they are bringing with them a message or an energy vibration. I'm not absolutely clear about this; I think it is energy. Apparently the race that they come from is known to have this special energy. I am hoping they're going to show us what this energy is, as it seems to have colour rather than form. Red and blue stand out, which are the different ends of our visible spectrum, aren't they?

Elaine: Yes. This shimmering wavering light that I see is like a very elongated oval, so I feel very strongly that there is a 'person' shape inside. And my feeling – and although I don't particularly like titles – is that there is some kind of group forming of one great 'Master' in the Light. I say those words, not because there is any pomp and ceremony needed, but because those are the words that I heard telepathically – and that *need* to be said when we speak about the vibration of this person or group of beings (whichever it is). I really feel that they normally have no human form, but now one entity or group being is taking form in there. I know I definitely need to 'jack up' my vibrations in order to capture whatever it is that it wishes to convey to me.

Ann: Yes, I feel this energy is something we both need to experience, and that it will help us not only now, but in the future, with the information that we hope to bring through. It's a different vibration from anything that we've been in touch with before.

Elaine: The light I see clearer now is multicoloured, like the kind of light you would see refracted from crystal, but very delicate and very fast moving.

Ann: Yes, It seems to cover the whole spectrum of light and colour. I feel that it's something similar to what we might call a 'cosmic' energy – but on a much higher vibration than something you would associate with the energy of this Universe. It's energetic, but now becoming like a material physical form. I have a strong feeling that we should just sit quietly for a moment, allowing ourselves to be immersed by it – and to feel this energy really deeply.

Elaine: Yes, I certainly feel like I need to be in a different vibrational state than I am now.

Pause: We now take a short while to sit with it and adjust.

Ann: I feel a pressure inside my right ear, and a slight high-pitched sound – but it seems to be passing now.

Elaine: Yes, that can sometimes be something to do with a change of pressure in the atmosphere. For myself, I have a slight headache in my third eye area, and I can feel that my heart rate is up a little bit. I also feel a field of electrical energy all over me, like the beginnings of a strong tingle, although it's very mild at the moment.

Ann: I am moving into deep space now, passing very fast through the paths of galaxies and suns, stars, and into a nebulous space where all is *absolute stillness*. Nothing moves – it's like a chamber of silence. And deep within this silence there is now coming a resonance.

Elaine: Yes! I am with you on that, I am there too.

Ann: And it's starting to build...

Elaine: YES! I hear it and feel it, like the deepest boom, but so soft and subtle.

Ann: Yes...very quiet, but building... And this resonance is filling this place we are both in, and from that resonance is now coming sound that we can understand as sound. Now that sound starts to move outwards of its own accord – or rather, that sound *has* to go out. It can't be contained. And then, things start to happen. It's finite matter that it is creating, but it's *so small...*

Elaine: Yes, I know you and I are seeing exactly the same thing. I was flying through the centre of a great dark wormhole, with all the glittering stars rushing past me and then I came out into the dark field, which was as you said – absolute stillness. Then my body felt the gentle sensation of the subtle boom of sound that suddenly was there – but there was almost no noise. That boom is now rushing straight towards me like the rays of the Sun – coming from the horizon of deep space – like a huge whoosh, or breath of wind and movement, in which everything is blown outwards and it blows *through* everything.

Ann: Yes...to me it seems as though this is the *beginning of finite matter* that is so small, so microscopic, that we have no name for how these particles exist. We have not discovered this birthing of matter, because it's not matter as we understand it. But it does become matter as we *will* understand it. And out of this seeming chamber of stillness or void, comes the beginning of all that we know to be – can we call it Creative Dust or Nebulous matter?

The chemical reactions that are created, along with the friction between these minute particles over eons of time, create a much denser mass which then becomes 'stardust'. But this is a very lengthy process of chemical reaction to create building blocks of matter, and we have no concept of that at the present moment, because to the eye it would be totally invisible. All there is, is this resonance.

Elaine: Like a big out breath or a sigh...

Ann: Yes! An out-breath of resonance that is so soft...

Elaine: But powerful!

Anne: So soft, and yet, powerful and palpable.

Elaine: Yes, I see that exactly Ann, I can really feel it!

Ann: I think this is what is meant by "The Word". You know, from the Bible – In the beginning was the Word?"

Elaine: Yes!

Ann: It's an out-breath...and how it comes to actually even *be* breath, in this seeming stillness, I have no idea! But somehow, *it creates itself* into this amazing flow of subtle, subtle energy!

Elaine: I totally agree. It's almost as if it drops in from some other dimension!

Ann: It births itself, and you can't even see where it comes from – it just appears.

Elaine: Yes! (We are both so excited to be feeling and seeing this together in exactly the same way).

Ann: It will go on doing that for ever, infinitely... And it's not within its purpose to continue on creating, without something else having to 'die'. The dying of star systems and the collapse of Galaxies is a natural effect of birth and rebirth. Everything has its time and its limit in that way. So there are always new star systems being created as an end result somewhere. But the end result is rebirth rather than death, with everything collapsing in on itself in order to be reborn, remade. And I'm wondering, if when a single star or star system collapses inwards on itself, if it actually goes into a void, like we've just seen, or does it create this dark chamber of stillness?

Elaine: Maybe that's what a black hole is?

Ann: Yes, maybe it could be. When I saw this dark chamber of stillness it was as if I had to go to the edge of the universe – and not necessarily to a dying star system. So I'm not really clear on that but I'd really like some clarity! There is this continuous flow of birth and rebirth, like recycling, or renewal. And what I understand is that every renewal and rebirth is essential for the Universe. It is such a lovely energy that they have brought tonight, because it feels as though it would be really nice to just sink into it.

Elaine: Mmm, Yes... Almost like you could do nothing except watch and float.

Ann: I can see so many light beings here, and they look diminished, as if they're a long way away in the distance. They look suspended, as you were saying earlier.

Elaine: Now I can also see – coming from this breath or source – a spiral. It's as if you were looking right down through the centre of a corkscrew, and I notice that it is light *spiralling* towards me now, instead of light coming at me in straight beams, as it was when I first saw it.

Ann: Do you know what this means?

Elaine: No not yet. Well, now the word I am hearing is 'motion'. Remember I said to you that it felt like the rays of the sun coming at me in a shuttlecock shape when we were in the stillness? All the rays were coming at me in very straight lines, but fanned out at all angles like rays of sun coming down to Earth through the clouds.

Well, now I notice that the rays are actually revolving, so as they begin spiralling – which starts with a revolving motion – it drags in everything around it into the circular motion. As it comes forward, it's beginning to cause all the fine matter to move in an anticlockwise direction, making all this energy start to turn.

Ann: Does that help to organise the stardust, or whatever is collected?

Elaine: Yes, I can see this directly head-on, spiralling towards me. And its shape reminds me of a child's toy Slinky, but with larger spaces between the spirals. I realise that with each turning sweep that it takes, that the dust or matter drawn in is spinning faster in the middle (like a vortex) but flows outwards to the spiral edges, and gets flung outwards in dense clouds at the outer edges. This is just like an Earth tornado, which picks up matter from the ground at the centre, then flings it out, as the tornado gets wider at the top. Also, when you have a turning motion, this is when spherical globules form as they are flung out. It's a little like the difference between tap water coming out of the tap in a straight line, and water going down a plughole. When it starts to turn and circle like that, it starts to speed up and becomes more organised.

Ann: Like a chemical or a molecular change?

Elaine: I think more structured. But what the beings are telling me is that when it spirals, it starts to create different speeds within it. So if you think about water going down a plughole, at the centre of the plughole the water is spinning very fast, but at the very outer edge its revolving much slower. So we then have various speeds of circular motion, and that adds an extra dimension to everything.

I'm now being shown something else. Imagine that large corkscrew shape. Now stand to the side of it, so you see the complete spiral from beginning to end, and whoever is telling me this shows me that when it is stretched out fully, it actually is a waveform! It's just like a sine wave, only instead of rising up and down on one single line, it spirals as well. They are trying to give me a good example – Aha! I think I understand now! What they want me to understand, is that sound is both a particle (which contains information) and a wave (sound in motion). So in the absolute stillness where we began, the straight lines that came at me at first represent this breath or resonance of conscious energy. And they are sound waves that encompass being both the container and organiser of the particles. The spiralling energy in the middle actually holds information as well. I don't know how I can put it that's easily understandable, but with the circular motion or the energy, this now has information content and organisation. It contains consciousness and meaning, like a voice coming through a large old-fashioned megaphone. The megaphone or container has straight edges but the actual spoken tones from the voice, and the meaning of the words, originates from the centre of the circular megaphone aperture or mouthpiece, and come out of the megaphone in a circular motion...as the spiralling wave form. I understand that they are probably explaining it to me like this, because I know about sound – and so I'm going to ask the question... What are we looking at here? Is this the source of all things? What is it?

Now I'm hearing them say: When everything ends, it implodes upon itself and forms an inner facing, spiralling 'black hole' (as you call it). The whole of this event is formed into, and becomes, a Torus shape. If you went *through* that Torus of energy and matter to the other side, you would emerge and be the source of something else.

To put it more simply, the Torus energy shape is continually going forward on itself, turning itself inside out. The inside becomes the outside...meaning that an implosion forms a Torus, and perhaps reverses polarity or becomes the opposite of what it was? And that event at the 'out-breath' on the other side, is an expulsion of resonant matter, that then forms into new denser particles as it spirals out, flinging droplets of particles into space as it goes. Where (in time and space) that new 'space' is though, could be another dimension, or a different frequency range, or something I know nothing about as yet. So, this place of stillness where things are created and suddenly appear is in itself, both the interconnected beginning and end of something greater. How else can I put it? They are showing me all sorts of multiple images!

Ann: Can you describe what they're showing you?

Elaine: At first they showed me a reptile, and then a snake shedding its skin to reveal a shiny new body. They tell me that everything which appears to die, decay and then disappear, is actually energetically imploding in on itself or condensing, and renews or explodes by turning the inside into the outside. A good example is when a human body dies and decays, the inner soul or energy emerges, and becomes a new form of itself in a higher dimension.

On a larger galactic scale, for ease of understanding, matter finally implodes where the process of re-birth begins, to be re-born as something of a higher vibration. The implosion creates a black hole or Torus shape in space. The mouth of the implosion becomes as antimatter, and then as the energy rushes through the Torus, it is a process of turning 'inside' out, (or shedding its old form), as the Toroidal energy flows in never ending circles around the central core. At the opposite open end, this is where you get the 'whoosh' or 'breath of creation' into a new dimension in space.

They're now showing me that you can see this in the microcosm and macrocosm – small and large – and they are saying that on one level there are many of these, but on the ultimate level there is only one. All the many are also part of the larger one. Do you understand what I'm saying?

Ann: I'm not getting the whole picture

Elaine: Well, say for example I could point out three billion black holes in this universe, which are small versions of what we are looking at right now. If you could imagine the entire Universe as an entity, that entity in itself, will eventually implode into particles of matter, creating a singularity.... then be drawn inside itself and pass or travel at speeds greater than you can imagine, through to the 'other side' and emerge as higher vibrational matter which will birth a new universe on the other side...... Do you understand now?

Ann: Do you think this new Universe would be in another dimension?

Elaine: Yes, I do. As I said before, I feel from them that the visual thing that's part of the whole process is Torus shaped, but also like a constantly growing fractal, in the fact that when a Universe does eventually 'die' and the whole thing implodes, it doesn't *actually* die, it turns itself 'inside out' and is reborn at a new level, by imploding through the Torus and emerging to birth itself as a moving sound, (particles of matter and moving sound-waves) which is the source of creation for a new higher vibrational dimension.

Ann: Yes, because it can't cease to exist.

Elaine: No, nothing ever ceases to exist.

Ann: It's like the envelope of its being, being opened out, transformed and folded back on itself in a different way.

Elaine: Yes! They also tell me it can and must happen (at a time we do not yet know of), on Universal, Galactic and Planetary levels. There are many energetic bodies in our Universe that are renewing, and eventually when everything has made the change, that's when the larger 'whole' will be ready to be re-born – if you know what I mean. But they say this is beyond our concept of time.

Ann: So the larger whole will represent our Universe?

Elaine: Yes and our Universe is one of many. If you can imagine soap bubbles, they say that our Universe is connected to – and part of – thousands of Universes, like thousands of connected light bubbles contained in the energy of All That Is. And then if they *all* eventually burst and turn into new matter, the bubble form would be gone, but the particles will remain. Those particles represent the wisdom, consciousness and intelligence of those Universes, but they now vibrate as a higher form of energy in a higher dimension.

Ann: So, it's the Universe being reborn? That's quite a big subject! – And hopefully is *not* going to happen right now!

Elaine: Oh, not at all – we are talking about it being beyond time, impossible to ever imagine!

Ann: I suppose you could call it infinity and that infinity is the time we need to change, as everything always changes and grows. Time as we know it is just something that we created here as a marker for days and weeks and years, etc.

Elaine: Yes, I'm being told that nothing ever ends; nothing is ever lost, as you cannot destroy anything. The shape and form changes as we as humans do in our incarnations, but the vital essence of who we are cannot be destroyed, because we are part of All That Is. Not even our bodies are destroyed really, because they decay and return to dust particles which remain, but in a different form.

Ann: Yes, nothing is lost, and everything changes – that's the feeling I had when I was seeing all those Galaxies dying. They all go back into this 'black' space, just being re-birthed into something else!

You could say that when that happens, that's their opportunity to be taken out of the set of dimensions that we're all in. Because I should imagine that what we see in the night sky has to be in our dimension, so that gives them the opportunity (even a whole galaxy) to be raised up into another vibration and dimension of existence?

Elaine: Of course, on the other hand, all the dimensions cannot be seen within the visual range we have, so another aspect of this to be taken in account, is all the other dimensions we can't see, including parallel dimensions too. It's all very complex!

Ann: Now, the question arises   knowing how big a galaxy is – how is that made to happen? That every single soul and created being in a galaxy, can be at the same point of evolution and spiritual evolvement (the same energetic vibration), so that everything is taken through at the same moment? That's awfully big isn't it?

Elaine: Yes, I think there's a saying that goes, you are only as good as the lowest member or denomination of your team, and maybe you have found the crux of the matter. Perhaps all our many galactic neighbours have just been waiting for us (as possibly the lowest denominator in our quadrant of the galaxy) to shift, so that everyone else can shift.

Ann: Well I know that way back in the 1960s, I was told that the Earth was the keystone, and that what happened with us – and what we did here – was that important that it affected everyone else in our galaxy and even the universe. We could hardly comprehend this, as we are such a small 'speck of dust' in our galaxy, but somehow, where we are going now, and how we're doing it, does seem to play an important role in our area of the galaxy. We could be the last ones to evolve, and that might mean that the entire galaxy has been waiting for us to ascend into a different dimension?

Elaine: Yes I think you may have hit the nail right on the head there! It's certainly a possibility.

Ann: It's an amazing thought. It gives a whole new focus to the future, and I think maybe we'll begin the process into a different dimension, but we'll still be able to inhabit physical bodies.

Elaine: They tell me now, that there has to be a balance between the levels of awareness of souls on this planet. And all you need is one featherweight more to tip the balance to the positive side, where we need it to be. It's as if we are at 50-50 point and all you need is 51 per cent to make the balance more to the positive, and that's the point we are approaching (this was in 2010).

In fact they tell me now that it *has* been reached, and the scale is coming down on the positive side. And so whatever is going to happen is inevitable, and this change or metamorphosis is in motion.

We are on track and we are in it now.

Ann: That's good to know.

Elaine: Yes, absolutely! I have thought very long and hard about the people who don't appear to be at-one with themselves, who don't have positive vibrations. Those people who are asleep, unaware, and continually perpetrate negative acts, such as those who fight all the time – and people who appear to be without any kind of kindness or compassion. And I asked the question, how does that equate? But apparently, I'm told, that when the balance is tipped by just a small amount, then it will all slide exponentially. The words I'm hearing are: There is no need to explain the intricacies of everything that will happen to everyone. Suffice to say, everyone will be where they are supposed to be, and order will remain.

Ann: I've been told that before, and I believe that too. Nobody will be lost – there will be a place for everyone. I think the real message tonight is that nothing is *ever* lost, nothing can really be destroyed. Everything continues on in some form, always with the purpose of it becoming better.

Elaine: Yes, exactly. And now I'm extremely aware that someone has superimposed their energy into my energy field now, as I can feel it over the front of my forehead. It could be the Sirian being that I know. I feel two large lobes in the front of my head, there above my forehead, with a very, very strong focal point being on my third eye. I can feel it from about the middle of my eyes upwards to the top of my head. I can't feel it below that, so I'm going to wait and see what happens.

Ann: Ok.

Elaine: The new energy settles, and I asked the Sirian Being: 'What will it be like on Earth after or during the changes'?

Sirian Being: Everything will be and seem the same, except every day will be a happier day; every day will be a joyful good day. This part of the change will be subtle and almost imperceptible; except that you will not remember the last time you didn't feel good! And things like sharing and having good neighbours will just happen naturally. You will unexpectedly find yourself doing it, having it, being it.

Ann: Can I ask a question? A slight diversion here, based on what we just said; I'm thinking about some of the young people that are on this Earth today, feeling quite aimless and dissatisfied with what the world has to offer, they seek pleasure rather than knowledge. Will they be able to move away from that reality while they are here, into a greater understanding? Will they want to learn wisdom, and gain spirituality? How can their lives change from what they are now?

Sirian Being: Ah...in unexpected ways. People such as you speak about – we say that when others respond differently to them, they will reciprocate in unexpected ways. When people begin to recognise and respond to the new reality that is forming around them, it will be like having a new toy in the playroom.

Suddenly their attention will divert to new things that interest them more. Everyone at some point becomes disillusioned with doing nothing all day, or allowing continuous self-indulgence. It's like having as many chocolates as you care to eat. Eventually, the day comes when you think, 'I don't want another chocolate!' And you begin to look around for what else is there. All I can say to you is that all things take care of themselves, even to those that can see no meaning to their existence right now. The new energy will affect those who are full of fear, and are desperately hiding from that emotional fear by indulgence or destructiveness. All things come to an end and pass away, allowing freedom to begin again with a cleaner slate.

Having said that, many of those who physically die and pass over will be allowed the option to remain in your spiritual realms for as long as is needed. This will be to learn their lessons and raise their vibrations before they can come back to Earth. The new higher vibrations of a more loving planet Earth will not resonate with some, and so they will take longer to return. The Earth will sing at a higher vibration and be karma free, as much purer souls without previously held emotional issues will match resonance and incarnate there. Those that really cannot resonate with the things that are coming will exit the world and stay off planet until they are ready to understand the level of vibration that will be needed in order to incarnate on Earth. Do you understand that?

So really there is no need for concern about those who may be near or dear to you, or that you have worries or concerns about. Your primary concern in this reality is to create and to extend your own 'breath' of creation, and your own word, as we showed you in the beginning. And from that, like pebbles in a pool, it will touch souls in your immediate surroundings, and their words will touch you too. You are the micro of the macro we showed you in the Chamber of Stillness in space, and you will begin by first creating your own metamorphosis. Your family follow, your neighbour next, and your country after that. Do you see what I mean? Only by each individual changing and becoming who they will surely become, will complete the vibrational shift.

Elaine: I am being shown cells in a Petri dish, and they are all dividing and multiplying until there are millions of them. When one divides, everything divides, and so our only real concern is to look within ourselves to change, because everyone else will have this agenda too, and each will deal with it as they see fit.

Sirian Being: And the results of all of this will be extremely evident within five years. The changes in people will have grown so much, that within five years there will not be anywhere in your world where you will not see it in evidence.

(Author's note: It's now 2017 and I see it happening everywhere!)

Elaine: I am asking him telepathically now: But there are still all the people who fight, and there are wars all over the Earth. What about that?

Sirian Being: These things will take care of themselves. As you rapidly speed up your own personal change (like the rapid division of cells on the glass), it will just grow exponentially. As you, who try to come from the heart, turn positively in one direction, those who cannot get to grips with this will turn negatively towards the other direction. They will go to a place of change for them, either if they have passed over, or are still here on Earth. They will implode inwards upon themselves and then be held in energy form until they can reach the same vibration of everyone else.

Elaine: I am now being shown (as a metaphor), two post-horns. A post-horn is a long thin trumpet, with one end being a wide circle, and the other mouthpiece end being narrow, small and circular too. You blow through it to make sound. I see two trumpets joined together at the large end (where the sound comes out), and we are now metaphorically *right in the middle where the two meet*. The people who are of a positive disposition will travel through the tube from the middle and out into a new dimension, a new way of being – and those not, will go the other way. But eventually we all end up in the space outside the trumpet.

I see it so very clearly in my mind. The people that have gone the negative way need to go through the process of learning and changing again until they match the new vibrations. It's all about vibration, and it's all about resonance attracting and vibrating at the same pitch, like attracting like. And within this, the only thing that you can ever do anything about is yourself. Good gracious! If you could film what is going on inside my head right now, you might be amazed. I am seeing so many things on multiple levels. There are holograms of everything, where every tiny part of the big picture *is* the big picture – like a fractal.

Ann: And these are holographic images of what might happen?

Elaine: No, everything that *will* happen. There is no 'might', as everything happens in the now, and they have shown us the biggest picture – the macrocosm. The silence and out-breath experience we saw at the beginning is the bigger picture of 'one whole body' – and now they're showing me one cell, representing the Earth, the people and everything – which is exactly the same.

Ann: So everything we see that exists is part of the whole bigger picture, and this bigger picture can be shown at every level – be it macro or micro – and it's still the same pattern of how things are?

Elaine: Yes, and he shows us our metamorphosis or shift, and we, according to this, have tipped the balance and now are about to change. The positive has prevailed and we are learning that we have the choice to be different. We are all now in the process of shifting a dimension. I can see it so clearly in my mind. Everything is changing and is going to change more. It will all be fine, but everything will be different, looking the same but feeling different.

Every person or thing which does not resonate with that will change and be recreated somewhere else. And in this case, they tell me it will be like another level in spirit. Instead of reincarnating again, they'll do it differently this time. They'll finish learning the lessons in energy form, and they will have to resonate at this new vibration before they can reincarnate back down on Earth and join whoever is down there. Does that make sense to you?

Ann: Yes, because I believe there are schools in the spirit realms, where souls can be educated. So perhaps for some souls that just can't get it together down here in the third dimension, they need that extra time to be educated in a place where things are a little bit better structured.

Elaine: This is a cut-off point, and if anyone has not made the progression to a more positive way of being by a certain point, the door closes and they have to change and learn somewhere else, in order to get through the door in the future.

Ann: I think that's quite possible. What's of paramount importance is that the planet itself has to evolve. Whether we all evolve at the same rate is not going to be the important part of the equation when the time comes, as it's down to individuals. And as you have described, those who haven't quite got to the point which matches everybody else, will be taken care of in that way that you described. They will be educated, and be in a different energetic realm where they can get the information and knowledge that they need in order to progress, because there will be no time left to do it on the Earth.

Sirian Being: Yes. And when they *are* born again, they enter the new vibration of a different Earth, where all karma, past lives, and difficulties of the 'old' Earth will be gone.

Ann: I see what is emerging from all of this. No more time can be wasted on 'karma' and reincarnation, it's all got to be finalised at a certain point in our time as we've all realised that enough is enough. No more 'rebound' effects with finishing emotional life lessons, or reincarnating endlessly to fix problems. This cut-off point is making way for a whole new world and a whole new way of life. I think that having no fear will be of paramount importance. We have to learn that fear can no longer play a role in our lives, and has no need to.

Sirian Being: Fear is on the other side of the scales, and you cannot take that with you!

Ann: I agree. Self-created fear is of the old world and the old life, and doesn't have a place in the new.

Elaine: I'm getting some amazing visuals on this; I wish I could capture them and show them to you. It's all being shown to me as a metaphor.

Sirian Being: You already have it written that there will be a new Heaven and a new Earth.

Elaine: I get goose bumps all over with that statement!

Ann: Yes, I'm really feeling that too! That's the way it has to be.

Elaine: I'm asking him, can you tell me more on how it will happen?

Sirian Being: I take you back to the very first 'out breath' in the stillness you saw tonight, when things seemed to turn inside out. You will not necessarily see the changes happen, but you will feel it. To use another metaphor for you to understand, it's like when you have a terrible headache. When it goes away you don't notice that it's gone, you just feel fine. You would only recall that headache if you experienced one again. So you might think – oh, I feel this pain again. It's a pain I had forgotten I ever had.

And so it is with this world and all its current extremes of emotions. You'll just glide into the change imperceptibly, and only when you sit quietly and think, will you see that you don't really remember the last time you felt cross or upset. You might wake up one day and ponder that you haven't had a 'bad day' for so long, you can't even remember what it feels like. You may even forget what a bad day was!

Ann: Yes! I was going to say just that, you might forget what it's like to be cross or upset.

Elaine: Exactly! We humans, with our forgetful minds, probably won't notice that it's not there anymore. If you never sneezed again, would you sit around thinking I haven't sneezed? No, you wouldn't!

Sirian Being: I repeat, it will be an imperceptible glide into the changes.

Elaine: Now my skull is tingling like crazy, and there are people here who are really close to me in spirit, and they are reminding me that this is one reason why we must all take time to be still and pay attention to the self.

Sirian Being: Each and every one of you can only really pay attention to your own self. If you are busy with your attention in someone else's 'process', such as being too involved in someone else's life or their business, then your own process goes untended. To take from your mind Elaine – 'Be the change you want to see'. So be peaceable, content, and happy. Love every moment, accept it and stop struggling. Stop, there is no need to fix anyone else – deal with yourself!

Elaine: Oh, now there are alarm bells going off in my head, as I'm thinking – I won't have any work to do if I do that! (I am a therapist)

Sirian Being: You must understand this too. I take another metaphoric principle from your memory. Imagine you have a spinning wheel, and you pump energy into it with your foot to turn the wheel. When you stop pumping, the spinning wheel does not stop immediately, it gradually gets slower and slower until it stops turning. So, do not think that when we say pay attention to yourself, that the whole world is going to change immediately around you

This metaphor of the spinning wheel, once again says: Do what you need to do from day-to-day, tend to your children and those kinds of things, and gradually you will find that the things that concern you so much with others will grow less and less, until the day comes when there is nothing to do but be happy. Do you understand what I mean? I do not mean you cannot be kind and helpful, or that you should ignore everyone in favour of yourself. I mean, correct the balance so that at least 51 per cent of your energy goes into having more awareness of yourself and what you are doing on a daily basis.

Elaine: On a personal level, I really see what he means. Can you see it Ann?

Ann: Yes, I can see it, and I do believe that. If you want to take the stress out of your life, do not allow your life to lead you so much, but let yourself move through the day with ease, and everything will happen at the right moment with little effort involved. Of course there is some direction of energy, otherwise you wouldn't even walk out the door! Everything will become organised without needing any stress, and I know it's to do with our conscious mind. If we put stressful deadlines to one side, and allow events to take their own course without interfering so much by saying what we all say...'oh I haven't got time for that' – or – I'd love to do this but I can't.

Sirian Being: I repeat again, the less you struggle, the easier it is.

Ann: Yes, a lot of joy can come with that. We all know when things start to fall into place, such as bumping into a person that you've wanted to talk to for weeks and haven't been able to reach on the phone. Suddenly it all feels right – the shopping gets done in half the time it usually takes, because your mind is focused instead of being led all over the place. This brings a certain kind of joy into your life because you feel good when things like that happen.

Elaine: Exactly! Do you remember what I said earlier tonight – that I had felt strangely happy for the last couple of days? It's not as if I haven't been working hard, but something has shifted within me, and maybe they helped me to feel that as an example of what they've said tonight. They approached the topic from the 'big end' down to the 'small end' as an illustration that not only is this happening on Earth, but also in our Galaxy, and the ripples go out into the Universe as an inevitable change occurs. And why? – Because this is a 'node' – a point of change for us. And that means the collective us, and maybe even the rest of the Galaxy!

Ann: It makes you want to ask the question, is the third dimension going to dissolve?

Elaine: No, it cannot dissolve, so they tell me – It has to be there.

Although, hang on a minute.

Sirian Being: Please don't confuse. When you speak about the third dimension in that way, there is more to say.

Ann: I see a notebook with blank pages: third dimension. When you start to write inside that book by putting words on paper, they have come from thoughts, which are not third-dimensional. So this is a metaphor for another aspect of the third dimension, the energetic aspect. Although thoughts and inspiration are recognised and seen to be in the third-dimensional world – they are not *of* the third dimension.

Elaine: He's explaining telepathically, that when you said 'Will the third dimension cease to exist' and I said No, he makes me feel that I could say No *and* Yes.

Ann: Yes, it's the way you perceive it – it's a paradox.

Elaine: It still appears as the third dimension we know, but it won't be the same. The *energy* will be different. It's like going up one octave on a piano, the notes are still the same but it's a different pitch than the octave below: double the original frequency. The qualities and consciousness that exist in the world as we know it today will become a distant resonance or sub-harmonic, and what we establish with shifting our consciousness and awareness up an octave, will become the new fundamental resonance. This then becomes our new physical reality, and as it grows stronger it creates its own energetic harmonic in the octave further up. This will be the vibration we will aspire to reach in the future.

Have you ever looked at 'cymatic' patterns, which are the shapes that sound creates in matter when played through a resonant flat metal plate? If you have, then you sometimes see a curious thing happen. At any given pitch and volume, sound will create a pattern. You will also see that the pattern can sometimes revolve in a clockwise direction. If you raise that pitch to a point just below the perfect octave above the original tone, you will see a kind of chaos appearing in the pattern. When the resonant frequency hits exactly the octave above the first tone, the chaos disappears and the pattern takes on a more complex shape and appears to revolve in the opposite direction. I feel that the chaos and war we have seen world-wide over the last years are like the example given above. We are just on the edge of a new octave, in a pattern of chaos, where everything seems to be getting worse and breaking down, but the truth is, that this is the precursor and signal that we are about to reach a higher more complex design.

This is also like a spiral. As it rises up ever higher, it flows to the right, then the left. But as it rises, it's always passing through a different place in time and space, even though the spiral is still intrinsically the same. It's a natural progression of evolvement. By being of service to others and showing both kindness and the courage to trust in the good in the world, there will be nothing left of that old way of control and competition that we resonate with. We will have moved on... and some say it will be a different timeline, like a parallel world. The world we know now will still exist, but becomes immaterial to us and unseen. The new higher frequency will be *where all our awareness is focused*, so becomes our new reality, and it will be as if the old never existed.

Elaine: I think we should close our connection now. That session was very reassuring don't you think? To feel that in essence, we needn't worry about a thing, and all we have to do is be very mindful, and be present in the moment. We can carry on with our lives, as whatever is happening is now inevitable, all is ok, because we are on course. But we must always stay positive, face any remaining fears, be aware of our thoughts and have an attitude of kindness to others!

***

CHAPTER 8

A Touch of Light and Freedom for the Spirit on Earth

Ann opens the evening with a prayer to welcome guests.

Ann: I'm bringing in loving energy to welcome all guests. May they know that here is an open door, for those guides to bring their insights, wisdom and knowledge for us to share. So we say thank you for what is to come.

Elaine: Thank you Ann. I would like to say, just before we go into anything deeply, that all my guides are *very* present in the room tonight. This includes a very strong energy of the spirit essence of Jesus standing over to my right. The Extraterrestrials are here too, and they are all standing still, waiting and looking in your direction, Ann. I feel they are waiting for someone to come in who is going to speak, and I'm not sure whether it will be with me or with you. But in deference they are looking in your direction.

Ann: I somebody with me now. What I can do, is just allow him in – if it's just a preliminary of what is to come – because otherwise I don't know what to do.

Elaine: That's fine, Ann – Go ahead.

Guide: Good evening. I bring many blessings on you both.

Elaine: Thank you.

Guide: We have listened to your conversation earlier, and we do sympathise, concerning how you feel that life is at this moment in time. How every day it seems – not difficult – but hard to get through sometimes. We would like to reassure you that everything is in place and in order, you need have no doubts. If there are any questions you would like to ask, I would be very happy to do what I can to answer. I have known this lady (Ann) for many years, and I will just fill you in briefly.

My name is Pierre, and she first met me when she was experimenting with automatic writing. This is not my preferred method of communication, but I think it was curiosity that led her to try it. She was encouraged to do it, and it surprised her when the greeting I always gave at the end of the messages, ended with one word – as she had never heard this word before. But opening up her Bible, she found it in the book of Psalms. And I think that made her feel that somehow, something outside of herself had been able to communicate – as she had had no previous knowledge of this.

Elaine: What was the word, Ann?

Ann: 'Sela'. Some of the Psalms end with that word.

Elaine: And what does it mean?

Pierre: It is an intimate word, not so much a farewell, as a loving greeting. As when you say, 'We'll meet again'. It has a lot of love attached to it, and is not final, like your word Amen, but is more like, 'Until the next time'.

Elaine: Can you give us any news from the spirit realms? Anything which you feel is important for us to be aware of now, and that we could share with others world-wide?

Pierre: Well, it is very busy in the spirit realms on all levels right now from the hierarchies down, and what people must understand – is that when I say the word hierarchy, it is not a level that creates a distance between itself and people such as yourselves. It suggests that there are many different levels of wisdom and understanding. With each level something different is learned, and is brought into the soul's heart and mind. There are levels where people cannot learn these things for themselves, but must be taught. There are also many levels where experience is given through knowledge being imparted in a very different way than the way knowledge is given on the Earth.

So it is not so much like a teacher/student relationship, rather an integrated understanding of what the wiser soul is conveying to the soul who wants to learn and reach the next level of experience. For example, the teacher and pupil would become an *integrated embodiment* of any knowledge that's being given. On certain levels, knowledge is shared through being at-one with the person who is giving the knowledge. This can be done in the form of matching thought resonance, sometimes with a demonstration, and then the knowledge can be conveyed to a new soul who seeks enlightenment. You could say that when you meditate here on this plane, you can sometimes reach a state of consciousness where knowledge that is quite new comes pouring through. This new knowledge can be mostly understood, but there is no preconceived notion of *what* you might be learning. This is when you have touched into a particular realm of learning through resonance, because your own energy vibration will have matched that of a being on another level, higher than yourself. This is what I mean by two becoming at-one, and embodied as one thought.

At the moment, on this spirit level, we are working very hard to bring this bridging-of-resonance more into being on the third dimension, where we can reach those who wish to learn through their meditation exercises. We can enable them to gain wisdom by direct contact with higher levels of being. In this way, knowledge is given to them in the purest form with no interferences. So we hope to keep developing this more, as increasing numbers of people on this planet wish to learn and become more aware. But as you already know, some people require more understanding of how meditation works.

They need to be able to place themselves in a safe environment, in a quiet room where there are no outer distractions. That is the only way we can reach them. Those people on Earth who wish to learn more for themselves and do not wish to go through a third person, should give themselves a time to meditate, and to be at peace with themselves. In your busy world, there is often little time left to be with yourself, away from distractions, and to practice this type of meditation. Many already use meditation in order to relieve stress and find some inner peace in their heart – without necessarily opening up their soul's capacity to receive inner wisdom.

We would like more people to do this now – to open themselves up to receive higher wisdom, by making a direct link with those in spirit who will bring knowledge to Earth in this way. This is also because we're now moving into the Age of Aquarius, and people no longer need a physical teacher. They can now access wisdom for themselves through meditation, and we actively encourage this step forward. We want people to consider this now, as it will help raise the vibrations of the soul and body.

Pause: A different soul comes in. A lot of white noise is heard on the recorder.

Ann's Guide: Peace be with you.

Elaine: Peace be with you too, and welcome.

Ann's Guide: It was essential to have that little talk first, which has enabled me to come forward. We wish you both to understand that there is a time coming soon which will be progressively different from life as you know it now.

(Author's note: This is happening right now!)

I want you to understand and prepare a pathway, not only for yourselves but for others. If you will, you can be a way-shower to help other people with guidance. If you say you are willing, then it must be so. There is no contract to sign, but we understand from the resonance in your force that you are indeed willing. This will necessitate much work for both of you, which is why we have to be absolutely certain that you know what you are preparing yourselves for. There will be great joy in doing this, so do not be deterred, if at times it seems too difficult to overcome certain obstacles. It will never be too difficult because we will always be there to guide and lead you, as this is something that needs to happen – and we need many people such as yourselves.

There seems to be so much to do in such a short a time. We are prepared, and we need the people of Earth to volunteer and also be prepared. We advocate – with your provision – that you try to lead a life that in every way possible is peaceful and disciplined – inasmuch as you do not allow yourself to wander from the path you wish to take. Once on this path there is no deviation, and the world as it is will always seek to distract you. Do I make myself clear?

Elaine: Yes you do.

Ann's Guide: So do not be distracted or deterred by what other people think or say. We feel that you both have reached a point where you will not be so easily distracted. You are both quite anchored, safely and securely in your beliefs, and in how you see your pathway spiritually. And we know that you both wish to serve, and understand you wish to do this in the best way possible, and the best way for you is following the path directly ahead. There will be many events on the way that will be tempting, but we ask you to be focused, and not to be distracted. Regarding those opportunities that may be very appealing, always meditate on them and think deeply about what you will do – then know and trust that what your heart tells you is right.

You can always ask for guidance because we will always be there – we always have been and we always will be, and always is forever. There is such a lot to look forward to, and I have to say that it is our experience that people who work with spirit on this planet of yours receive the greatest joy even with the toughest troubles they have gone through. Is that not so?

Elaine: Yes indeed.

Ann's Guide: So, if you find things becoming tough, then you must understand that the joy that will be at the end of it all will be sublime. Do not give up, do not be deterred. We will make sure that the rays of the great cosmic sun that holds true love, true enlightenment, true joy, will always be surrounding you. All you have to do is to trust that it is there, and tune into it when you have need of it.

This essence that comes from the cosmic sun is available to everyone. We do not pick and choose, but we see light from people from where we are, and we understand what is in their hearts. This is when, like a beacon, we are called to come closer. And, you cannot imagine the joy that there is in the celestial realms, when that love has found a true heart in which to dwell. Then the whole planet – for that brief moment – lights up. The tiny spark is ignited, and the Creator sees that another soul has joined with the forces of light with the essence of joy. That joy will never leave the soul that has experienced the light. As that light is so strong, it lays down an anchor in the true heart, and never lets that go. Once that link has been made, it will never be broken, so trust that with all your heart.

If you could see the colours that surround this planet when people send out their love, meditate with true sole purpose in simple joy, or pray – as many people do pray – you would realise that it changes the colours around your planet, and the Earth vibrates with these harmonies.

I know you often wonder why you have wars. This has been a planet of conflict for a very long time. But gradually the planet herself understands that it no longer serves to have that unbalanced energy, and that it needs more love, joy, and light in its energy field. And gradually war will die away. It will no longer be in the planet's consciousness, and that is why we need more people to understand how *they make the difference*. Every individual on this planet makes a difference, and we see it happening now.

I must now go, but I thank you for listening.

Elaine: We thank you for coming. We are very honoured to have you speak here this evening. Thank you for your wisdom.

High pitched white noise is again heard on the recorder.

Pause as another guide comes to Ann.

Guide: I come from the race you call the North American Indians.

Elaine: Welcome!

Guide: My name in your language is Raining Storm; as when I was on the Earth I loved the rain, and the energy of thunder and lightning suited my character. In those days I was a warrior, and I had to learn how to become a peaceful Warrior. I wish to say that my people in America are now working hard to bring back the old traditions of working with the land and with nature. They call on the mountain spirits and the spirits of all the elements. I would ask you to say prayers for them. America is going through great upheavals and there will be more to come.

(Author's note: This is happening right now in 2017).

It is necessary for all people to get rid of the dross that they have allowed into their lives, the unrealistic desires for their type of perfection, which no longer have any spiritual basis. It has been a big tragedy for my people for many decades, even centuries, but they have tried to keep the faith.

I have here in my hand, a pipe of peace, and I offer it to you.

Elaine: Thank you. I accept most graciously.

Raining Storm: May I ask – if you have tobacco, please give some to this person (Ann) and take in the smoke as if you held the pipe of peace that I offer.

Elaine: I will do that, thank you. I take it with much gratitude.

Ann: And please keep us in your thoughts.

Raining Storm: We will. And no matter what you hear about my people, only believe the good; because they *are* good, and they have had much to deal with. They also are reaching a point where all separate tribal differences will be put to one side, and they will learn to be a brotherhood again – One Indian Nation. That was always the dream. Great Spirit wanted us to be one nation and not many, nor to be fighting each other – and it took the white man to change that. So in some ways, it had to be so. There is no blame, no blame at all. And now the tribes must meet and come together as One Nation, so my prayers would be that you give strength to this dream.

Elaine: I feel it is a dream that we could follow by example for the whole world. Every country could come together with their own individual gifts, talents and traditions, and we could be one Nation of Earth people.

Raining Storm: I think if my people could start the ball rolling – that would make me very happy, yes; because you must have noticed how, in the last decades, everyone wants to split off into their own little country, and remove themselves from each other, and it is not good to do that yet. Patriotism of that kind does not help. It's good to know your own culture – yes, but don't put out boundaries or borders. However, the time will come when this will end. But first, we take a moment to smoke the pipe of Peace.

The blessings of the Great White Spirit be upon you, and Mountain Goat as well. Very nimble he is, and can see the whole picture from where he stands!

Elaine's Guides: I feel I must just say something at this point, because my guides are coming to say that there is a reason and a purpose to individual countries becoming split apart from the whole. And this is a good reason, because over the last millennia, years, or whatever times in the past, the governments have become too big. They have collected states and collected countries, become unions and commonwealths, who all then come under the rule of just one government.

Whilst on the one hand, it was initially good to be a brotherhood of one nation, in the end, what came from that were all-powerful, corrupt, infiltrated governments. They became distanced from what the people truly needed, and no longer listened to the people. They ruled instead of serving the greater good. One ruling government can never be diverse enough, and becomes too big and out of touch with all the differences of culture and ideas. You will find, if you look back in history, that all the great empires – because they grew too big – fell and crumbled away. And so what are the good things that come from small countries or states becoming independent?

First of all it may seem that they are becoming strangers to one another and very 'anti' one another. But you will see in the end, that this initial stage is because huge establishments of grand government (where responsibility of governing so many people lies with so few), always become corrupt at the very least. Some, who are honest in government, never have their day – never do you hear their voices –

because the weight and pressure from those who would control, has been too strong. But before things can be reborn into a new form they must break down completely. They must first divide and give the power of choice back to the people. To allow – for example in America, the states of Hawaii and Texas and those other states who wish to be independent – allow them their independence and individuality.

The same is with your government (Elaine and Ann), in the United Kingdom, that when your government fails to be united within itself or Europe, then let it ask the people from all sides to speak their own truth. We say this, because eventually, when power is focused more on smaller areas, and is handed back to the real people, then this movement – that has been growing since the beginning of the 1960's – this power will be for peace and love, and honesty will become the driving force that governs. And it will be collective and not monopoly-governing, not somewhere where just a few people command all the money and resources. It will be smaller collectives of many people across the Earth who will all contribute to the whole wellbeing of the planet. And then this is when you can become a United Nations of Earth.

There will still be delineation and recognition of nation and culture, and that whole movement will take some time to manifest. What we must see is partnership and sharing, and a giving of power back to the people from the business corporations, from the giant companies who dominate the way things are done, and are now beginning to fall to their knees. The right to choose belongs with people who promote things which are good for the Earth and its people, and not for the money it gives them. So, we say to you, there is a blessing on those who first separate out and say, I must do it for myself.

If, in the United Kingdom, your areas of Wales and Scotland or anywhere else wanted to be separate – recognise that they do have their own languages and culture, and yet they are all one from the same island – as an island, it will all eventually coalesce, and the strength will be in the people knowing their roots, not in just being classified as British. Remember what the name actually infers, that you are a united kingdom. But also recognise that there are differences from the north to the south, and each person is equally proud to be who they are. And then the power to speak freely, and the power to choose and make decisions locally will come from the people.

In the same way, our Extraterrestrial brothers who wish to help have found that it does no good to speak directly to governments who would hide the truth and manipulate people. We have found that our best entryways are directly to the people dotted around your planet in every single country. In every place on Earth, we are connecting, offering help and guidance. And you have formed your own network with your loving hearts and your messages such as that which we give today. So that web of companionship, commonality, and joy, is both the webbing and infrastructure that keeps that foundation strong.

Structures that become too tall will always topple, so when governments rise and become bigger and stronger – detached and higher above the people, they must fall. But a strong foundation on the ground will stay forever. So, do not be concerned, because all is as it should be, as our friend spoke of earlier. Everything is in order and all is on track.

Ann: So do you think that our North American Indian friend was actually looking at the bigger picture in the distant future, with no borders and no boundaries?

Elaine's Guide: Yes

Ann: Yes, that's what I thought. That will take time to settle in.

Elaine: Yes. When he spoke of all the tribes becoming One Nation, this, in a way, is a future scenario for Earth. Where all countries retain their uniqueness, but above that recognise that we are all beings from Earth, and each part of the whole is respected for what it is. If the tectonic plates on the Earth shifted in such a way that all lands came together again, and we were once again (as we were many millions of years ago), one landmass surrounded by ocean, there would have to be a different level of thinking. And, believe me when I say, there *will* come a day when there are no borders. No more passports, no more walls dividing ordinary people, because things will occur on the Earth to bring everyone together in equality.

Ann: Yes, I myself see that as the direction we need to go on this planet. Towards an end result where there is loving harmony, where we can still all be individual, but all work together for the good of the planet. After all, it's the Earth that gives us all a home, our food, and the air we breathe. That would be wonderful!

Elaine: When there is a huge necessity, then necessity becomes the mother of invention. When there is a great need (should a natural catastrophe strike), usually there is a need to open all borders, to forget differences, and to save people's lives.

Ann: I really feel that people want to get back to their cultural roots because they seem to have lost that. What *does* provoke a question in me is this. There has been so much movement with so many people from different cultures, going to live in countries that are not their original country, that there are now great mixes of races all over the world – especially in Europe. So their customs and loyalties are changing, (*or not*, as the case may be) especially when they have children who are born into the new, adopted country of their choice.

Elaine: This is a part of a changing view of religion, and what it really is. I notice people around me complain and are distressed about the difficulties of accepting those of certain beliefs, especially, and in particular, the ones with radical ideas that are so filled with aggression and hatred against fellow man. We must remember that there are many religions in past times that have been guilty of attempted persuasion by force, believing that theirs was the only path and way of thinking that man should follow.

So on the first wave of any change, there will always emerge the 'bully in the playground', who would come in and say 'I want this playground for my own, doing things MY way – but they will eventually discover that behaviour like that only alienates them. What everyone really wants is to enjoy life, play and be friends with everyone else much more – but initially, the bully doesn't know how to do that. They have not been taught that if they do not wish to be judged, then they need to allow others to be who they are without judgement – and not impose their way on anyone.

I think you will find that as the years pass, the children that are born into different cultures will see and love the freedom that a lot of the world allows and enjoys. This has happened with immigrants who have come in from, for example, India. They are now so much more integrated into the new culture than their parents, growing more liberal, and really desiring and needing peace to enjoy themselves and be free. I hold the hope that this will happen within all religions that hold their followers in tight chains of obedience to their rules. Not just one religion, but ALL religions that have grown in power and control, becoming too tall – like a tower – too big and too controlling for their own health and growth.

Ann: And too rigid?

Elaine: Yes. Believe me when I say, we are in an age now when people's actions and words must be transparent. So anything that does not vibrate at the highest good for all, will be clearly seen and must change.

And in the light of truth and the light of change, the voice of people will say... No more! We cannot trust, we cannot believe in this, and they will once again look inside their hearts for what is real and what is really true.

Ann: I think that's the crux of the matter for me, when people start to think for themselves by looking into their own hearts, rather than looking to someone else who they think knows more than they do as a leader – one who is actually not interested in making another's real life any better, but is only interested in their own personal needs and wants. People need to take their own power back in a quiet and peaceable way, seek to understand for themselves the pre-requisites for a good life, and not leave it to other people to tell them what those prerequisites are. They need to understand that they can work it out for themselves instead of letting some other person do it for them.

Elaine's guide: Yes, there came a time once in the history of France, when such a thing happened with royalty and peasants, and brought about the French Revolution. It happened because those who were in power and were rich and comfortable had closed their hearts and minds to the people who starved, in poverty. People of Earth must have a revolution now (which means a 'turning around'), but it must be a peaceful and harmonious change, as balance in power, resources, food and health must return to all. When you raise your vibrations to enter a new level of being, you cannot make that shift when there is an imbalance in the scales. In order to transition smoothly you have to let personal balance be something you work towards steadily.

I can tell you now of an example. When you look at a pair of scales it may still be more heavily weighted on one side than the other right now. But if you take a small portion from both sides, then balance that small portion, that balanced portion can go forward and make a pathway for all the rest. It will happen in stages and in waves; and it is those who have balanced their differences already – those who have looked with new eyes at their religion, their gurus, at their governments and media, and said: This cannot be the way forward. No, I will follow no more, and I will look to my own heart to guide me with kindness and courage.

There are people right now who have made the balance work and are leading the way by example for the rest of us to make the transition. And it is inevitable, it absolutely *will* happen. So whilst you witness war and upheaval around you, do not worry that it will never end.

IT WILL.

And possibly sooner than you think; even now the soldiers of the United States, the United Kingdom and many other countries, really wish to withdraw from areas of war and strife. You are all feeling that none of you actually wish to be part of any further conflict, and are now seeking graceful ways to exit, because such is the nature of the age we are in. You are all feeling more and more strongly every day that you must find peace inside. You long to be in the country, in the fresh air, following simple pursuits, doing the right thing, having honesty, truth and openness as your banner.

 And so it will be.

Ann: That's good to know. Thank you. I feel that there are so many people here with us tonight, and they *all* want to say something.

Elaine: Yes. This feels like a very 'homely' night tonight. All guides and visitors very closely packed in the room.

Ann: Yes, and I think some of the Extraterrestrials have come to listen as well. They don't necessarily want to come forward and speak, although they are quite capable of doing that. Just being very polite and quietly listening.

Elaine: Like a progress check. I sense an energy amongst the Extraterrestrials that is feeling very pleased to be witnessing the things already happening. Because what the guide spoke of just now, is already happening on Earth. It's a flow that will gain momentum. We will see rapid changes around the world (including America and England) and then other countries will build on that momentum.

Ann: Momentum and change starts slowly and then becomes like perpetual motion. It starts to increase in a very natural and flowing way. Once it's built up, the vibration of the energy will carry it forward. I get confirmation from one of the Extraterrestrials that this is how it worked on his planet, and how his planet had to go through these kinds of birth pangs, after having once been a very warlike, disturbed society. He says that over long periods of time the people changed.

It wasn't a very populated planet, and that there had to be a working out of what was good for the people. And the people finally grew spiritually and realised that war was not good for them, and basically, they told their leaders so. They said, 'Come on – we're not stupid you know – war is not good for us or the planet!'

It took a bit of hard talking to those who governed, and some of the leaders had to step down and let other people come in to take over their role. Then people made choices for themselves, and yes, it took time. But he is saying it can be done, and they have proved it can be done.

Elaine: I feel very strongly that if there was no 'foreign' presence in some countries where there are wars now (and this applies to everyone on Earth), and we just let the people of that land learn the lesson that they must learn – and that is to say no to what they feel in their hearts is wrong, and not be afraid – then things could, and would, be very different in the end.

Ann: I think that the pure, original (untouched by man's translations) religion is all about peace, and there are those who have lost sight of that with perhaps an imbalance and dominance of male control in some societies. Not all the societies that are religious, but the ones we hear about most seem to be male-dominated. It has tended to err on the side of the 'warrior protecting his people' rather than erring on the side of the male nurturer who wants to follow the tenets of their spiritual leader's scriptures in its truest form.

Elaine: Ann, I'm being nudged to say – take a look at English history (or any other country's history for that matter) and see how male-dominated English history has been. Remember that not until just about one hundred years ago, did women start to become truly on their way to emancipation. I remember that we had Emily Pankhurst and the suffragette movement at the beginning of the 1900s, but we British (in perhaps a less violent way) also expected our women to cover themselves up and not show themselves. Everyone wore long crinolines or skirts, and we also felt that women should not be educated in the same way as men and not have a vote.

Ann: Exactly.

Elaine: Even back in the Middle Ages as you know, although there were occasionally strong women who could look after themselves, most women had to rely on the men to provide, to have a paid job some way to earn money, and to take care of them financially. So only in the last sixty or so years in the western world, have women begun the process, and are still calling for equal recognition and equality with men. And maybe this is all it would need – if we left countries alone, such as those that are at war – to find their own balance.

As we progress into the future, modern women (and modern men!) will protest about inequality. There will come a time when we all realise that we are all equal in worth, we just have different roles to play and jobs to do. I feel the lesson for anyone in this position of inequality, anywhere in the world, is not to be afraid. We are all learning and growing, realising slowly that we all need each other, but still need to respect our own individuality. And whilst we still wage war, even if it is thought to be a 'well-intentioned' war, this can never be.

Ann: I remember some women in African history (not so long ago). These clever women of a warring village decided to take away their husbands 'right' to have sex, and they said that if there were no more male children, they could not be taught to fight or forced to go to war, to probably die! Because all the women worked together, they were quite a force to be reckoned with. And of course, if there were no more children, then, they said, it was better that their tribe died out, rather than go through the sorrow and pain of losing husbands and children in constant, stupid wars.

Elaine: The truth of it is, that every soldier, terrorist or vigilante is someone's son or daughter – and surely no mother would want to see her children die or to be killing someone else's child. And what is it all for? Because some government, religious leader or tribal chief has got mad at somebody else, and then asks his people to fight for him and justify his anger? Without a doubt, the biggest futility on Earth is war.

Ann: I think the moral here is, if we work together peacefully with anything we want to change, we can create the resonance for peace, and when all are in harmony with it, you can change your reality to anything you desire.

Elaine: I agree, and now I feel that the energy around me is fading and that enough has been said on the subject. So I would like to say a big Thank-you to all of those beings who came tonight from different places and dimensions, for giving us information on different areas tonight. This is certainly food for thought for everyone. Ann and I are extremely grateful. What an interesting evening!

***

CHAPTER 9

Joy to the World, the balance is tipped!

Ann opens with a Prayer:

Ann: We thank all spiritual guides and Extraterrestrial friends, and welcome their energies into this room. They are all very fond companions, and we know their wisdom will be helpful to us tonight. We ask that they bring the essence of higher knowledge, and energy that lifts us into a moment of grace. And so, welcome to all.

Elaine: For some reason, I feel very excited tonight!

Ann: There is someone here who I have never come across before. Her name means Radiant Beauty. I know nothing about her, and she brings with her a wonderful energy. Her name makes me feel that she expresses energy, beauty and radiance in herself, in her persona, and that the whole sense of her being is to bring beauty into people's lives and encourage them to create beauty for themselves. As she gets closer, I see that she looks Oriental – Chinese I think. She tells me that she lived on Earth a long time ago, and is just coming in briefly to say *Hello*, bringing her beautiful energy into our room tonight, while she observes.

Elaine: Welcome to her. I'd like to say that my guides have changed positions tonight – the ones who stand on the left of me have swapped places with the ones who stand on the right, so they are all in different order around the room. They form a circle around me tonight and are surrounded by every single Extraterrestrial that we were in contact with when we worked on the first two books.*

* 'Voices from our Galaxy', Elaine Thompson; 'How Love Works', Ann Matkins.

Ann: Yes, I see them too. That's interesting!

Elaine: It's very unusual. The Andromedans come regularly, and occasionally the others, but not *all of them at once*. I do still have this tremendous feeling of excitement, joy and almost jubilation, that something wonderful is happening, is about to happen, or has happened already. It's like a feeling of joyous relief, which makes me really feel so good!

Ann: Yes, it does feel good. I see old friends coming back tonight as well as new friends. I'm glad you said that, because I was wondering why I can see all these familiar faces.

Elaine: They tell me that the event we are all waiting for has begun in earnest. And they are all so pleased that everyone is on board that should be on board, and that we are now on our way. Now what that means I don't quite know, but it just feels like a great celebration. The feeling of joyfulness is extraordinary!

Ann: That's wonderful. We must be doing something right! Have they given you any inkling as to what the celebration is about?

Elaine: I think it has to do with the balance of energy on Earth – you know, between negative and positive? I am told the good future-paced positive energy has outweighed the negative, and it has now enabled a lot of things to fall into place. I know we've heard about this before, where we all have to be consciously positive and so on in order to make 'the shift', but they are giving me the reassurance that it's done. The balance has really swung to the positive, and we are on our way.

Ann: Good!

Elaine: It's like a metaphor, where we are sailing on a boat, we've cast off from shore, and all we've got to do now is enjoy the ride. And they tell me the boat knows where it's going! And the good point is that we actually made it *on* to the boat, and didn't get left behind!

Extraterrestrial: The balance of consciousness on Earth has now come out in favour of the positive; therefore no one actually gets left behind. The energy coming in takes everyone with it, in larger or lesser degrees, but there is no one that is left out, not involved, or not influenced by it.

Elaine: For most of today, and even more right now, I've had a great feeling that all our Extraterrestrial brothers and sisters are now gathering so much closer to us and to Earth. It's like they've just gone another mile towards final communication and introduction, as we have taken a huge and deciding step closer to something amazing.

Ann: They have become our closest friends. It's a feeling of companionship that I haven't actually felt before tonight. It does seem to be like old friends meeting, who will always be friends.

Elaine: I'm now seeing strong visuals of those fourth-dimensional crop circles that appeared this year, and the interpretations that were put out. They were all about how the Earth is passing through a wave; that the wave is changing the frequency of the planet, and the effect is going to be profound. Just as was shown in those four crop circles, there will be varying degrees of integrated change. And even though it's going to be a tremendous change – it's so subtle – the way the edges blend, it's almost imperceptible. It's like seeing a boat sailing off, without a ripple or wave anywhere, and the water is like glass, so its smooth sailing. Remember the things I spoke of last week, about suddenly realising that you always feel happy?

Ann: Suddenly you think, well what do you know? I've been feeling very happy for a long time now, and I seem to feel really joyful every day.

Elaine: Yes!

Ann: The joyful message from the Extraterrestrials is that everyone can have that feeling – it doesn't cost anything, it's a state of mind, or rather is more a state of heart – the heart-mind. Oh, and I'm still feeling that some of our North American Indian brothers are here tonight as well. They've come in to remind me that last week they asked us to send out our good wishes to them, because they feel they have a purpose now to make a difference in America. But they still need help to get that energy working, and building up. They are even more positive than they were last week, feeling happier and more confident. They say that they can really do this, and be the movers and shakers in a good way, to help change the mindset of people – where people allow themselves to see the riches of the Earth and how nature and Gaia looks after them – that seems to be the big message!

Elaine: I see them as being great spiritual teachers for all the American people, because they remember the great wisdom of their ancestry when it comes to communicating with the elements, nature, and with the wise ancestors, lovingly sharing their spiritual nature with all people in the form of guidance.

Ann: I was meditating yesterday, and saw that if you go into nature and meditate, or just be quiet and at peace (which we must now think about training ourselves to do in earnest), it will give you the feeling for the wholeness and connectedness of the nature we are all a part of. We are not removed from it, nor separate from the energy of the planet – we are a part of it. We have mistakenly tried to separate and remove ourselves (quite successfully) from nature, and now is the time to return to it, and to feel all the atoms and molecules of energy around us in the air – and also the energy of nature spirits. We are totally part of that moving vibrational energy field, even though our human form is vibrating at a different rate, nevertheless we are still all connected.

Elaine: I am being told that as the Earth breathes, so we breathe, and as she warms, we warm, and as she cools, so we cool. So it's like becoming one, in a synchronistic blend, with Nature and the rhythm and heartbeat of the Earth.

Ann: Yes, absolutely.

Elaine: I feel still so excited tonight, isn't it amazing?

Ann: It feels exhilarating, and it doesn't seem to go away – it's staying with us. It's a bit like the United Nations of space has come down tonight and wants to share with us.

Elaine: I'm going to ask them if there's anything that any of them want to say, because at the moment, all I'm feeling from all of them are just these huge waves of joy!

Ann: Do any of your guides want to speak? I know you had the presence of the spirit of Jesus with you last week, does he wish to say anything?

Elaine: Yes he's here. I'll find out. But there's one thing I need to tell you before I tune in again. When I saw the spirit form of Jesus this week, he has doubled in size, so he is extremely tall tonight, way past nine or ten feet tall, with extremely expanded energy, which took me by surprise. So I'll just give it a moment and see…

Jesus speaks:

I am expanded because of the love I feel…which grows daily on this planet. Whether it is in the love between a parent and child... the love of the beauty that people see in others, or the love of being alive, it is growing. And hope is growing – and the day when all will be revealed is coming closer. This wave of love becomes all-consuming as it builds, and as it consumes, it leaves an Aura of Grace wherever it passes through. And the Grace is a permanent mark that never fades, so when you have loved or been loved, when you feel love for others and act accordingly, not only do you add to the transformation of this world, but you magnify the Grace for yourself and for others.

When I was seen to be resurrected, I was resurrected by the Grace, and you too will feel as if born again. You too, will feel the awe and the joy of realising the depth and breadth of who you really are – the soul within the body. So it is a joy for me to tell you that this day is a day of celebration, because the 'battle' is won, if you would call it such a thing. Mankind's battle with himself has been to change the patterns impressed upon him and generated by him, over the millennia. And so I say to you – give thanks – because what is done is now done forever. It stands in Grace and cannot be undone.

Elaine: I have asked him now, what was it that tipped the balance? And I'm given a picture of a soldier in Iraq, and I think he is an Iraqi soldier. And I witnessed a moment of absolute compassion…a moment of grace that he gave someone that was about to die. And in that amazing moment, he spared that man, that person …because his heart said: No. And I am shown that this act of compassion was that last feather that tipped the scale.

Ann: That's all it takes – it's wonderful.

Elaine: It's like a whole mountain of people changing slowly, but it took that last 'breath' of weight to tip the balance. And now I see that vision so clearly…I see a bombed windowless building made of clay and block or even just clay (I can't tell) and I see a man with his hands tied behind his back, bleeding, on the floor – with a soldier who has a gun aimed at the side of his head. And all it took was a look – a look from one's person's eyes to the other, and it touched this soldier's heart – and he chose not to kill. And from the man who was about to be killed, the thanks that he gave to his god and to his maker – and the relief and joy that he felt – those heartfelt feelings combined. And in that moment, in that situation…Grace filled the room.

Forgiveness and compassion: I see a scene in Africa now where someone who has money, has gold rings on his fingers, and is wearing a suit – is giving a child a piece of bread. And this is a symbolic thing. I feel that those who have plenty – more than enough – could so easily give such a little amount to save so many people, out of the compassion and love in their hearts. Now I'm being taken to China: I see those in government, and I'm being shown the thoughts in their minds, the sleepless nights and the conscience that troubles them concerning the things that they do – which they know they shouldn't do. The Persecution of Tibet and Tibetans comes to mind.

Now I see people in places everywhere around the world having a twang of conscience, thinking twice about whether they can live with themselves if they continue to do what they're doing. And my goodness, I really trust that what I'm seeing is actually happening right now. I *know* that Jesus is showing this to me, and it's like (as we spoke about before) this wave of energy is triggering the energy of love. Well, maybe not absolute love initially, but it's a complete energy that enters the heart and from it comes the thoughts of ....'Should I really do this?'

And questions arise. You feel those questions inside, when you know that something that you are doing hurts someone else. I'm also being told that along with those feelings – the central point that's coming to a lot of people – is that it's not about money anymore, it's about, 'Can I live with myself?, How do I feel?'. And perhaps this huge waveform that I saw engulfing the Earth, and that is pictured so beautifully in the crop circles, is the trigger for these little changes I'm being shown.

I remember being told some years ago by the Extraterrestrials that they were placing a sound-wave grid around the Earth – pouring frequencies down, in order to help modify our anger and our rage, so maybe these things have been working and working, and gathering strength? And now that we've arrived into this quadrant of the Galaxy, and our solar system has moved into a position where we are encountering something that we can't even see, or don't know about – that's part of what is activating this change worldwide. I'm being shown Iceland now, and the steppes of Russia; Australia, and the Amazon forests. I see just about everywhere, with so many people thinking twice about their actions.

Oh my goodness, this is amazing – if what I am seeing is true. And I really believe it is, so that makes it even more wonderful.

Ann: So it's a wave of energy that is passing across the Earth through us all?

Elaine: Yes, and when that wave is accepted and those people make the right choices then the Grace grows stronger. Thank you for that.

Ann: It's wonderful, and very reassuring. Now I feel somebody here, and they just want to say something.

Ann's guide speaks: The message that is coming tonight is to give you all reassurance, and to make you all aware that in all things and in all ways, you are never left on your own. There is always someone, something, some spiritual energy within reach, that is there to help you move forward into the bright new future that the world can expect soon.

Nations are finding their own identity at the moment, and it has been a struggle for them to do this. But it seems that they need to know their true identity before they can reach across to their brother and sister countries, and say: Let us shake hands. Let us get to know one another as we truly are. Not as our politicians make us seem, but to know each other as we truly are, which is as human beings who share the same lessons, the same trials, the same wonders of everyday life, as well as the same moments of having to make decisions – difficult or simple – whatever they are. Let us remember that we are all on the same journey, and therefore everyone on this Earth has the same right to be helped. To be in the moment and feel this powerful energy just described, and to truly know that this wave of Grace is passing across the face of the world embracing everybody in its love, is a wonderful gift indeed.

What people are beginning to be aware of, is that very deep inner heart wisdom that has always been there, and now has a chance to come up to the surface of people's consciousness. That soldier was actually touching into what his heart was telling him, his heart wisdom. It was not his mind. But when you look into someone else's eyes and you speak from the heart, then all barriers come down. You find deep communication without words. And it's that sort of communication that is going to work the best in the future.

There have been enough words, some of them very hurtful to each other, but now a new path is being taken, where people are willing to meet together equally. And maybe meet as the Quakers do – they meet in silence, and only when it is felt deeply does anyone say what is in their heart, if that is appropriate. And in that way, each person can be heard at the right moment, in the right space, having awareness of each one's rights, so that it becomes more of a brotherhood of nations, meaning mankind as a whole. This is what all of your friends can see tonight – the beginnings. The seed has been sown and it is growing fast. Now watch it grow!

Thank you for this opportunity to come and meet with you both, and join in the spirit of joy that is here tonight.

Elaine: Ann, do you know who you have been speaking to here tonight?

Ann: I don't know if I can quite get the name, but this person is from another realm, and his name is something like Atennier. (Aten-ee-ay)

Elaine: I have a feeling that his name has the same vibration as the name Mathew. I don't know what that means though, he just felt as if he was a soul who was close to Jesus in our time line of history.

Ann: Yes probably – it was definitely a male.

Elaine: Ann, I know this sounds strange, but I cannot remember what the date is today – do you know? Because for me, it seems that whatever the date is today – this exact point in time is extremely important, and it's probably no coincidence that we have met a day earlier than we normally do.

Ann: Sunday was the seventh, so today must be the 10th August.

And now I would like to offer our most grateful thanks to all who came tonight. Plus I offer a thought about the Persids meteor shower or shooting stars that are coming tonight, as it feels like it is a celebratory firework display!

*****

CHAPTER 10

Angels, the Sound of Earth and the

Connectedness of all Planets.

Ann opens with a prayer and welcomes all our Guides. She asks all Extraterrestrial friends from other worlds to join us this evening, and we thank them in advance for coming this evening, to share their knowledge with us.

Elaine: I'd like to speak just for a moment, Ann, as I feel something is different. I can't feel any of my guides close at this moment, and as well as that – as you were saying the opening prayer – I am very aware of an Angelic being standing right behind you.

Now I see another one standing to the left and one to the right – and one is behind me. So we have four Angels here in the room, on the four cardinal points: North, South, East and West. Ann, the one standing behind you appears to be sending out a huge amount of love, and smiling down at you, but up until this point, I can't anchor any of my guides in, nor can I anchor in any of the Extraterrestrials. So I will just have to wait and see what happens, but I have a very strong feeling that the Angels have come to *sing* to us for some reason.

Ann: Wonderful! May I quickly tell you about something that happened to me this morning that hinges very much on the quality of sound? I was meditating, and was taken down into the Earth to a chamber or cave, deep within the Earth. The cave wasn't hot, it was just normal temperature. In the cave there was a magnificent crystal – a white Mother crystal, and it had one very large crystal point that was set within a cluster. There were beings there that were very much like Angelic beings, but I presumed they were devic, perhaps linked to the crystals or with the Earth. They told me that the Earth has its own sound. They asked me to listen to it, and although it wasn't audible, it was a sound that I could feel in my entire body.

So, the Angel singing to me reminded me of what I saw in this inner Earth chamber, where the devic beings were also singing their sounds. They told me that the rocks and crystals that formed the chamber also had a sound, and they (these beings) represented that sound. They further told me that our planet functions perfectly when the sound that comes from its innermost core can reach out to the surface – to its crust – without any disturbance. But because there is huge disruption and disturbance on the surface of our planet, it affects the internal order and resonance of the planet.

Elaine: This resonance is like the beating heart of the planet.

Ann: The Earth is balanced because this sound is always a constant part of its fundamental being. The planet is always giving out this unique sound, and the large crystal I see is part of how this sound is created. Then I was shown another crystal, which was an enormous ruby. At the time, I wanted to say that it was a white ruby, but I was told no, it's not a white ruby, it is red, and it also has its own resonance. I was asked to stand very still, and as I stood there, I could, after a while, feel the resonance in my body. (Although I couldn't say I could hear the sound with my ears). As I think about it now, I am told that the planet can keep in balance with what happens on the surface, if nothing upsets the resonance of its sounds.

But we have been mining, drilling, fracking, having wars and blowing things up, which resonates down into our Earth, and the planet can only tolerate so much of this. Because this has been going on for a very long time, this brutal noise needs to be adjusted – and to do it, we (the people) need to start becoming much more aware and tuned in to the Earth. We really need to understand how sound is so vitally important to the way we live on the surface of the planet.

So to keep Earth more stable, the predominant sound has to be the pure sound that's born inside and of the Earth, and not over-ridden by the sound that we create. So we must be aware of, and understand the planetary resonance. They say that some sounds we create are beautiful (music, singing) and we mustn't stop doing that, but alongside all of that we must become more aware of what is beneath our feet. There are all sorts of sounds that we are unaware of.

Elaine: Yes, indeed.

Ann: And when we, in our everyday lives, hum or sing a tune, we actually do contribute, and help in some way to make our awareness of the planet a deeper experience. So they want us to go on singing, making sound and chanting, even with musical instruments – but it needs to be harmonious and not discordant.

I am told that a minor key doesn't have to be discordant; it really can be a beautiful sound because it's more of the Spirit. A major key is more of the Earth, but the two can be used. Both generate what we need in our lives to help us build a safer more joyful life. A life of more self-awareness that brings us back into balance with everything that the planet is and wants to be for us, so we can work in unison. I feel that this is the next level of our spiritual education. Yes, we want to work with the Earth, but not only work with the soil, work with the energy of the Earth combined with our energy, and this can be done through sound.

Elaine: Many years ago, when I lived in Glastonbury, I was also taken on a meditational journey which took me to the centre of the Earth. I too, saw all these wonderful massive crystals, and the devas or the spirit beings that embodied the crystals. They also told me about the resonant frequency of the Earth, and how the planets communicated with one another through their resonant sound and electrical fields. They showed me that all the planets in our solar system and beyond, had awareness of each other by the sounds and the energy that they emanate, like a neural network.

I am prompted to tie this into the changes happening now, and the fact that both the Earth and our solar system will also change in vibrational frequency. In simple terms, things are not only happening due to the power of our Sun, but also because of an even bigger influence, which the whole of our solar system and this quadrant of our Milky Way Galaxy are going through right now. It could be possible that there is some hidden truth here that has to do with the power of sound, I'm not quite sure. But I noted that the Angels here tonight are looking down at you with very loving eyes whilst they sing. They are singing into the top of your head, maybe to facilitate some change? I can't be sure.

This reminds me of the coded music that came from the Hathors which we downloaded onto our computers a while ago, giving us the pineal and the heart sounds from the future – which were apparently different from the present resonances that we feel today on a daily basis. It indicates to me that a shift in frequency is happening both externally and internally to us all. I have this great feeling of expansion.

For example, if a ball were to grow larger, it would need to be flexible in order to loosen its molecules so it could crack open, and expand. This is like a baby's skull as it is being born. The bones are not tightly knit, in order that they can expand and contract with the birthing and growing process. As the baby grows the skull expands, due to the loose knit spaces in between the bones of the skull; then eventually solidifies into the right shape to accommodate the adult brain. It feels like the Earth needs to discharge energy using volcanic activity and expand by cracking open with earthquakes. The Earth certainly could crack apart on the surface to allow for expansion from within, and then be able to generate the next octave of frequency up, or maybe reach the first higher harmonic of the resonant frequency that it is generating now.

I think the prime frequency will always be constant, but how purely it rings and how strong the harmonics it gives off is perhaps a changeable thing. And, as we are on the subject of sound – think about the added effect of gamma rays, solar rays, photons and the many different particles and things that are coming at us right now from the Sun and space. These rays don't just come at us and all bounce off the Earth's magnetosphere, they pass right through us and the Earth, and out the other side. They are tiny particles that pass through everything, and as there are millions of them streaming through us and the Earth every day, we are now subject to the effects that these streams of different particles have on us.

I feel that no one has yet discovered or identified just how many different particles there are, and of course when friction happens (that is when particles pass through you), they make their own sound, changing your vibration. They make an inaudible sound which can change, enhance or magnify anything within our physical and energetic bodies, as well as our world.

So that's the feeling that I get from what you have said so far, and it just reminded me of what I have been told previously by my Extraterrestrial friends. But I still have no clear direct communication verbally from my guides tonight.

Ann: When you were talking about the solar system, like you – I remembered that it was also mentioned to me this morning that all the planets in the solar system have their unique sound. I am now thinking that when all the planets in our solar system hit the right note, something major is going to happen, but they all have to hit a harmonious chord.

Elaine: Yes, perhaps all the planets in our system will come into harmonic alignment.

Ann: Yes, and so each tone becomes the next harmonic with the next planet, and they make up a chord that sings out to the Universe?

Elaine: The rest of the Galaxy perhaps?

Ann: Well, it certainly will be a very important moment when this sound is created!

Elaine: Yes. Because not only will we send out our new sound to all the other planets, but all their changed sounds will come back to us and resonate – then send that sound out and beyond to our local star systems.

Ann: I agree. And when I think about all the native peoples of this Earth, and how important their music and sound has been to them, it all makes a lot of sense. They have always chanted, sung or danced in a particular way to honour nature and the Sun. It seems to fit with how the planet needs harmonious action from us, so that not only do the sounds come from within the Earth, but we create a harmonic on the surface of the Earth in both a physical and energetic way, and somehow that helps to keep the planet alive, happy and healthy. I'm beginning to get a feeling that this makes total sense, and it can't be coincidence that so many native peoples who have never had any communication with each other, have always had similar traditions of chanting, singing and dancing.

Elaine: The thought comes to me too, that we (the people) are in reality a minority on this planet, with the majority of occupants of

137

this planet being animals, plants and trees, grasses and flowers, and that each one of those has their own natural resonant frequency.

Ann: One which we can't hear audibly, but together they make their own special sound – the sound of Nature.

Elaine: Being in tune with nature in order to be happy, suddenly takes on a whole new meaning! If nature in its entirety is singing the major sound or song of the Earth, then it's up to us to harmonise with that. If you think about the resonant frequency coming from the centre of the Earth, then the plants and trees on the surface of the Earth are a conduit for that frequency, and add their own melody to it. So, therefore, we must be in tune with them in order to join together in harmony as it were. Because *we* are the alien beings – the Earth herself, and the plants and animals are almost one. They are singing the same song because they can sing no other. But we as humans sing our own song. And whilst our own song can be lovely – if we became more aware of our roots and our connection to the Earth, I think that our song could then be in *better* harmony and be more in tune with the song of Earth and Nature.

Ann: Yes, intrinsic pure melody and sound is very different from just noise. And I think we've created a lot of awful noise on this planet, and it's not helpful at all with anything!

Elaine: Definitely not – and that's because we've been creating noise without any awareness of the background sounds that we live in, and are greatly affected by. I think this is a lesson in true reconnection. Remember when we were talking about wanting to live somewhere where it was green and beautiful and be in tune with nature?

Ann: Yes I do, and I think that the beings who are with us tonight have been listening to our desire for getting out into a greener environment. I know that anything and everything is possible if your desire is strong enough. It can certainly make things more possible and easy, if you just *believe* it. If I could be living with nature in a greener environment than I am in now, I know that every day I would feel that I want to sing my own song. That's not necessarily singing out loud, but feeling a happy resonance within myself that's in tune with the Earth, and with all that grows on the Earth, myself included. I want to be in tune with myself. And who's to say that can't be possible?

Elaine: Yes, you just have to make it so.

Ann: Well, I really do thank the Angels tonight for their guidance and for singing to us. When I was in the cavern in the inner Earth, the beings I saw there were so strong and tall, as part of the natural world within the Earth. And yet, they were beings of light, filled with luminous light and grace.

Elaine: And all crystals emit their own peizio-electric energy too, with quartz having an especially strong pulse.

Ann: Do you know, there was something special about the ruby crystal. It had a very earthy feel about it – a very strong, deeply powerful energy. Would that have a different vibrational pulse?

Elaine: Yes, it will be a different resonant frequency.

Ann: Earlier, I felt my North American Indian guide with me, and I'm not sure if he wants to say something now – do you have any more to say on that subject, Elaine?

Elaine: Not really, but I will just say that as you were speaking, there is something happening, up to my left in my internal vision. Deep space has opened up, and I have just seen that the most beautiful, elegant starship has arrived. It's a shape that I've never seen before. It's very elongated and luminous, and it's just hovering there. I've not contacted anyone, so if you want to communicate with your guide, I'll wait to see what develops with me, if anything.

Ann: I'll see if Raining Storm wants to say anything.

He is showing me a totem pole. I'm asking why he's doing this, and I think he wants to speak.

Elaine: Good evening – you are most welcome.

Raining Storm: Good evening, and thank you for your good wishes. I'm pleased to be here again. I was showing the totem pole to Ann because this was, and is, a very spiritual connection to make with the Earth, because what we carve into this totem pole are representations of the spirits of the Earth, and the spirits of the natural kingdom around us. It was used as a conduit to the Earth rhythms, and this is what we would dance and sing around. It was our focal point, so very sacred to us. Our singing and dancing would penetrate into the totem pole and carry that sound down into the Earth. And our prayers went with it, so that we blessed and thanked the Earth for being the Earth; and for the care that it took of us, providing all that we needed.

There is so little thankfulness in your day and age for what the Earth gives. It would be so good if people encouraged more of this to happen. I know that there is a strong movement in many groups around the world for doing precisely that. So we are very pleased about that, and applaud any movement towards creating this link with sound to the Earth. You understand that all American Indian tribes stamp their feet in the dance too. We believe that the sound and reverberation sent into the Earth carries a message with it – a message of recognition – that we knew the spirit of the Earth, and we would talk to it through our feet. All of this was held sacred to us, so when you plant your feet on the ground or you take off your shoes and walk on the bare earth or grass, be conscious of the fact that the Earth knows you, and knows what it is that you do. Everything, as you are fully aware, is interconnected. Every movement on the Earth's surface is known by the planet's soul. Everything.

I can see in your future that there will be a greater understanding of the negative activities on the surface of the planet. This impinges on everyone's lives in a much deeper fashion than people understand now, because of your intrinsic interconnectedness with the planet. Much negativity has to be swept away, positive action will be retained, and it will be good when people understand they are not alone. The starship you see is an indication of the help that will be received. We knew of our space brothers when I lived on the Earth.

We welcomed them when they came, but they were not there all the time. When they did come, they were all greeted warmly – as they were our brothers and sisters from the stars. I know there are many blessings here tonight that you have created, and all of us here tonight would ask that you remember that blessing. Take it into your hearts, so that when you leave and go about your everyday lives it will always be with you. And in the days to come, hold that blessing in your heart and know that all is working out in a good way for your future. Be very positive about your future. Do not doubt or give up; do not be saddened by negative thoughts of others which are less understanding of what is, and is not, possible. Stay true to your path – for that is what we wish. Here again I offer the pipe of peace, and our blessings from the Great Spirit. Thank you for allowing me to speak tonight. Good night.

Elaine: I accept the peace pipe, thank you for your wise words, and good night to you.

Now, Ann, I would like to come back to the star-ship that I saw just now. Right now I can see what appear to be blue beams of light coming from it towards the Earth, and when I say coming towards Earth – I can tell you that they are a long way outside of Earth's atmosphere. This feels like an indication of monitoring Earth from a distance. Their position is not as far as the Moon, but maybe half as far. They are fairly close, but far enough away to be able to see the complete sphere of Earth. I feel the multiple beams are facilitating some kind of transmission of energy. I've not seen this starship-shape before, and it's completely different.

Ann: Can you describe it?

Elaine: Well, it's very long. If you imagine a mandolin standing up on its end, it's that shape: an oval, deep shape at the bottom, tapering into a very slim long neck. Obviously not like the big bowl-shape that there is on a real mandolin, but more like a teardrop. At the very slim end, it splits into three or more separate lines, similar to a trident. Where the neck joins the body, it splits into two outside pieces, sweeping back around to join onto the main teardrop, two-thirds of the way down. The huge teardrop has missing parts either side of the middle section which leaves a long slim piece down the middle. I've never seen that shape before.

They tell me that their purpose in being here, is that they've come to watch Earth – and that again feels like something is very imminent. Whether they are going to be watching something which is invisible to us, I don't know. Maybe it's a change in the sound of the Earth, such as we were talking about earlier on, or maybe it's a change in vibration that changes the colour around the Earth? Whatever it is, they have arrived to witness the event. I don't think it's going to be for just one day – more stretched over a period of time. And as I have been told so many times, their time vibration outside the bubble that Earth is in, is very different to ours. So what may seem like a short time for them is maybe two years for us – I really don't know. I am now being given a visual of a baseball arena with the seats rising up to the top of the arena in a big oval, with the baseball square on the bottom.

I can see lots of beings and many starships arriving over time, like an arena filling up to watch what goes on from a far enough vantage point to be able to see other planets as well. I see the Sun, the Moon, and Venus – and I'm being told that it takes them very little time if they want to move over slightly and look at Jupiter or Saturn – that's not a problem! So they are taking in, and could view the whole solar system if they wanted to. But the main area of interest – where possibly the most events and biggest spectacle will be – is Earth.

Now I'm being shown waves of sound and iridescent colour. I've seen pictures of planes passing through the sound barrier on the internet, and they get surrounded by a cloud or mist as if they create some kind of dimensional field around them, and I think that's what they're coming to view here on Earth. Now I'm told that there is going to be an important event happening that makes all the rulers of all countries on Earth come and gather in one place. They tell me that on this starship, are all of the important people from many different planets. It feels like a Galactic Federation meeting, with all leaders gathered in one place, but I don't think for one minute that *all* representatives are here on this one spaceship, because our own Galaxy is so vast. I feel that there would be a spaceship, or even a fleet of spaceships, just for one quadrant of our Galaxy, so this may be just a group representative of our local area as it were. It's very difficult to say, as our Galaxy is so big. But they are trying to give me an impression of the size and the vastness of it all. We have no concept – no idea really – of just how big our *own* Galaxy is.

And still my guides seem like they are on holiday tonight, as they are definitely not here. I get a whisper of them, but they seem too busy doing something else, and even the Extraterrestrials who usually come aren't here. Of my guides, the only one who is here, is the Angelic being who helps me with healing – and she is behind me. She's one of the four Angels here tonight, and right now I'm going to spend a moment listening to them to see what they are saying. I want to know if there is anything else, or a particular message they want to tell me. In response to that, the Angel speaks immediately, saying:

Angel: *If you pay very close attention, there will be a flash of light as we bridge the dimensions, and suddenly the Sun will shine inside you as well as outside.*

So at all times, be aware that on the day this sudden flash of light appears, it will be like this:

And she's giving me a beautiful image of passing through the skin of a soap bubble into the next bubble. As we break through the skin and it closes behind us, there is a flash of light everywhere – in every single place, all over the Earth.

Elaine: I thought it was so beautiful when she said the Sun will come out and shine inside as well as outside – what a wonderful way to describe it. She says we will be passing through a barrier into the next dimension and individually becoming more peaceable, happier, and more loving – and what will do it, is just a subtle change to positive connectedness within people.

Ann: It wouldn't take much effort.

Elaine: No. If everyone, everywhere on Earth felt happy inside, there would be no thought of war, no thought of fighting, and no reason to pick up arms or even spend money on arms and weapons, no reason at all. Those negative thoughts of fighting would die in an instant, and we would then realise that there's more than enough to go around. There's more than enough money, more than enough of everything. And I'm prompted to say – just look at places like Switzerland, who remain neutral and are both rich and peaceful. I know this seems like a poor analogy, but it's the only one I can see right now. What the Swiss people can do – everyone can do! I know the key to it all is waking up every morning feeling good-natured and happy, and full of love. For myself, I can't wait for this moment to come. I am really, really *moved* by what the Angel said to me just then. And now I can feel something on the top of my head and across my forehead.

Ann: Yes, I can feel it too across my forehead.

Elaine: It's like a hand – a light touch – and I'm feeling that *everything* *is going to be fine, everything will be okay.*

(We sit in blissful silence for a while...)

Elaine: I don't think that there is any more that they going to say this evening. But I was just loving that perfect moment. It was like having my head held by an Angel, and it was really beautiful. So I give grateful thanks to all those that have been with us tonight, and a Thank-you for the information given. And we'll meet again soon.

***

EPILOGUE

It's Not Over Yet!

Ann and I met once again the following week in her cosy home in Glastonbury, not realising that this would be the end of the meetings for quite a while. She had broken her toe and was feeling tired and unwell, and I had been considering taking on some past life regression work. Little did I realise what was ahead of me! This account is a short synopsis of that last session with Ann.

We opened with a prayer, and invited out friends in for the evening.

Elaine: I have something to say, just for a moment. One of my Extraterrestrial guides that came in earlier on, has just returned and says: 'You're not finished yet – there is more to be written'. But having said that, he impresses on me quite strongly, that there needs to be a gap between any more sessions, I assume of at least three to four weeks.

He mentioned the ceremony you're going to do tonight Ann, and then showed me the past life work that I am thinking of doing, and tells me that the both of us will have to shift up a level, as whatever it is he needs to have come through me in the future, is at that different level. So he says that we are now done on this level, and the two of us have to get on with raising our vibrations to the right level in order to receive any further information.*

*At this point, we didn't really understand what this meant, and we both thought that it would be a break of no more than four weeks. How wrong can you be?

My pathway led me to a much desired change of house and location, but it came all in a rush, took me by surprise, and it all happened three weeks before Christmas, just before 2012. It was snowing, and I had to do all the packing, cleaning and preparation alone. It was both traumatic and wonderful in the end, and pushed me into facing and dissolving a raft of very human fears I was holding about not enough money, fear of authority, direction in life and personal survival. And last but not least, I had to jump into the unknown and step up my level of trust to the reach the *Absolute Trust* level.

So it was now 2012, and before I started to reconnect again, life swept me along on another amazing journey yet again. My intended visits to Ann's home faded behind all the new and exciting events that fell on me out of the blue, and Ann's life took twists and turns she had never expected.

And, as promised, the next level of information arrived as:

Raising Consciousness – Preparing for Change

Part Two

The Solar Effect on Humanity and Earth.

***

147

Printed in Great Britain
by Amazon

66039364R00092